THE
CANNON
FAMILY
GENEALOGY & HISTORY

John Cannon
John Cannon
Archibald Cannon Sr & Jr.
John C. Cannon
George Washington Cannon

Compiled and Researched
by Lanette Hill
Brightwell

Brightwell Enterprises, Inc.

INTRODUCTION

Civilization had its beginning around an open fire. Here at its warmth gathered the family group to find safety, comfort, and companionship. In tracing the word "fireplace" one finds it definitely related to the Latin word "Focus". There is the explanation of what home has always meant; for home is the center of life, no mere residence of the body but the axis of the heart; the place where affections develop themselves, children love and learn, where two toil together to make life a blessing.

Ones ancestors are the flagstones that have led to the home you now have. As each babe begins a new life from the warmth of a mother's lullaby to the adventures of adulthood, the days slip away as each flagstone is set in place; some carefully, some hastily--but all record the path, it seems to fade and become obscured in the distance. It is hard to visualize the battles fought, the seas spanned, the wilderness braved, deserts walked, fields cleared, houses built, homes made and families loved and raised--each event a stone in the path unseen on the other side of the rolling hills.

I saw behind me those who had gone, and before me those who are to come. I looked back and saw my father, and his father, and all our fathers, and in front to see my son, and his son, and the sons upon sons beyond.

And their eyes were my eyes.

As I felt, so they had felt and were to feel, as then, so now, as tomorrow and forever. Then I was not afraid, for I was in a long line that had no beginning and no end, and the hand of his father grasped my father's hand, and his hand was in mine, and my unborn son took my right hand, and all, up and down the line that stretched from Time That Was to Time That Is, and Is Not Yet, raised their hands to show the link, and we found that we were one, born of Woman, Son of Man, made in the Image, fashioned in the Womb by the Will of God, the Eternal Father

Generation No. 1

1. CANNON FAMILY[1] HISTORY

Notes for CANNON FAMILY HISTORY:
THE FIRST OF THE CANNON FAMILY TO ARRIVE IN USA.

There are other researchers who state that he spelled his name as Kennon initially; however in the actual records in Virginia the Ship Passenger lists has the name spelling as CANNON. JOHN CANNON There was another John Samuel Kennon who later changed his name to Cannon; but that Rev. Samuel Kennon/Cannon lived further up north in the Boston New York area and no connection can be found to our Cannon family line except that he changed his name to Cannon instead of Kennon once he arrived in USA.
.

The Cannon family moved from their homeland of Ireland due to the grievances and war on the land and initially traveled to England. Upon arriving in England they decided to leave and first settled in Barbadoes as a Planter before coming to USA. The Roy O'More is one of the families mentioned that traveled with the Cannons during this time in history.
.

Those on the Fortune were families members who had been left behind in England the year before or from the Netherlands.

CANNON, JOHN - arrived at New Plymouth USA on 11-11-1621 in a ship called "The Fortune". John arrived in America unmarried and was still unmarried in the year 1623 at the Divison of Land that year. John Cannon was single and was the only Cannon listed on passenger lists of ship. The Fortune was mostly a cargo ship and so there were not that many passengers aboard. The Burthen: was 55 Tons. It carried 35 passengers aboard.

He traveled on a ship named "The Fortune" financed by Thomas Winston who also financed The "Mayflower". as seen above. This ship was carrying the Simmons who hailed from Lyden, Holland and the the ship embarked from England to USA. Thomas Carton was the Ship Master. "The Fortune" means [chance or luck]. The ship landed in Plymouth, USA a few weeks after the First Thanksgiving.

It is suggested that he came from London, England. [more research to be done on this information.] My speculation at this point is that his ship did indeed embark from the ports of England; but the name Cannon and his family were from Ireland and of Irish descent.

In the 1623 Land Division of Plymouth; the listed has JOHN CANNON listed as a Planter of the Commonwealth. John Cannon is listed with a William Tench and they had two draws [probably because they were both single and moved to land together to work the land]. The other men listed that received the LANDS THAT LYE TO THE SEA; EASTWARD; were: William Hilton one draw; John Winslow one draw; William Coner one draw; John Adams one draw.

John Cannon and William Tench are seen alligning themselves with a John Billingsley in early records of the colony. John Billingsley later turned out to have charges brought against him in the Colony. John Cannon and William Tench left the Colony sometime after 1623 but definitely by 1627 as they are not found in records after that date. It is speculated in the history books that they either died or left colony.

On Plymouth Colony records John Cannon is listed; but he is one of those who either died or left. Since there is records of John Cannon from Barbadoes initially settled in Charlestown Virginia; it is posible that these two John Cannons are the same man. The dates and times are certainly matching as further research continues to be researched and found in history books and records.

Child of CANNON FAMILY HISTORY is:
2.   i.   JOHN[2] CANNON, b. 1642, Arrd-1656 Barbadoes/Lived in Barbadoes until 1660; then Livd Charles City Co. VA to Henrico Co. VA; d. 1695, Henrico Co. Virginia/WILL 2/1/1696-97.

At this point in this book there has been a great confusion as to the JOHN CANNON of Maury Tennessee. Was he the son of Archibald Cannon Sr.?
In March 2010; JR CANNON telephoned me and told me of a DNA testing that he had done. The DNA test clearly showed there are two different men named John Cannon and their information has gotten mixed up by researchers in the CANNON line.
This is an official email message received from JR Cannon explaining the facts concerning the JOHN CANNON men.
Sat, March 13, 2010 9:54:57 PM
From:
J. R. Cannon <jr.cannon@aircanopy.net>
View Contact
To: L. Hill <madisoncowgirlfan@yahoo.com>
Hi Lanette,
As you know, with genealogy there is always good news and there is bad news. Right now, I have no good news – only bad news. And it is that my John Cannon is NOT the son of Archibald. I could not find your source that the John Cannon that died in 1831 in Maury Co., TN was the son of Archibald. How can I be so sure? DNA

I am the co-admin for the CANNON DNA project at Family Tree DNA. I checked and sure enough, we had a descendant of Archibald's test with us. I compared his DNA with my group's DNA and found that the genetic distance is too great for us to be related. It just happens that he lives in Dallas, about 30 miles from me. I will be contacting him to verify his research.

I really hate to be the bearer of bad news just when I thought I was on the verge of a major breakthrough! But that is genealogy for you. So you may want to delete the descendants of John son of Archibald because it is incorrect. Even his death date of 1831 in Giles Co., TN is incorrect because that is my John Cannon's death date.

Anyway, I want to let you know. I will keep in touch and hopefully, I will overcome my brick wall.
J. R. Cannon

At this point in this book of research I want to include JR CANNONS John Cannon research on his branch. Once JR Cannon makes his connection to his John Cannon's father; I will update this book.

After his research; this book will continue with the JOHN CANNON line that settled in Georgia; and South Georgia areas.

Included now is JR CANNON's research on his line of John Cannon of Maury Tennessee that eventually settled in Texas.

===

Appendix # 1 through #4:

Generation No. 1

JOHN[2] CANNON *(THE JOHN CANNON - TENNESSEE TO TEXAS[1])* was born 03 Jul 1774 in North Carolina, and died 1831 in Giles Co., Tennessee. He married HANNAH.

Descendants of John Cannon

No. 1

1. JOHN[2] CANNON *(THE JOHN CANNON - TENNESSEE TO TEXAS[1])* was born 03 Jul 1774 in North Carolina, and died 1831 in Giles Co., Tennessee. He married HANNAH.

Notes for HANNAH:
John CANNON, b. 03 JUL 1774 in NC. He married Hannah _____, married 05 AUG 1793 in GA, b. 02 JAN 1774 in SC, d. 1856 in Maury Co., TN. John died 00 MAY 1830 in Giles Co., TN.

I.   Sophia CANNON, b. 11 JUN 1795 in Wilkes Co., GA. She married (1) John FAIRES, married 18 JUL 1849 in Maury Co., TN, d. ?. She married (2) William T. AUBRY, married 18 JAN 1860 in Maury Co., TN, b. 1809 in VA, d. ?. Sophia died AFT 1860 in TN.

II. Henry B. CANNON, b. 18 SEP 1797 in Wilkes Co., GA. He married Anna RICHARDSON, married 06 APR 1823 in Maury Co., TN, b. 1800 in Wilkes Co., GA, (daughter of John RICHARDSON and Syntha WILLIS) d. 1846 in Harrison Co., TX, buried: 1846 in Harrison Co., TX. Henry died 1860.

   A. Sally L. CANNON, b. 1830 in Maury Co., TN. She married Marshall BRASSELL, married 17 APR 1852 in Harrison Co., TX. Sally died ?.

   B. John S. CANNON, b. 1830 in Maury Co., TN. He married Mary H. THOMAS, married 02 JAN 1851 in Harrison Co., TX, b. 09 JAN 1833 in Maury Co., TN, (daughter of William THOMAS and Lucy CANNON) d. 22 FEB 1896 in Italy, Ellis Co., TX, buried: 1896 in Italy, Ellis Co., TX. John died 1860 in TX.

      1. William Henry CANNON, Sr., b. 12 DEC 1851 in Upshur Co., TX. He married Sarah Katherine "Kate" FORTUNE, married 16 JUL 1881 in Ellis Co., TX, b. 13 MAR 1864 in Peoria, Peoria Co., IL, d. 21 OCT 1950 in Eureka, Navarro Co., TX, buried: 1950 in Italy Cem., Ellis Co., TX. William died 27 OCT 1929 near Italy, Ellis Co., TX, buried: 1929 in Italy Cem., Ellis Co., TX.

         a. Eunice CANNON, b. 1883. She married Bernie Johnson FEW, married 1898, buried: in Italy, Ellis Co., TX. Eunice died 1954 in Dallas, Dallas Co., TX, buried: 1954 in Dallas, Dallas Co., TX.

         b. Richard Edgar CANNON, b. 18 NOV 1884 in Italy, Ellis Co., TX. He married Maud Ella HARPOLD, married 19 DEC 1909 in Italy, Ellis Co., TX, d. 22 FEB 1970 in Dallas Co., TX, buried: 1970 in TX. Richard died ?.

         c. William Henry CANNON, Jr., b. 01 DEC 1886 in TX. He married Eva BROTHERS. William died 17 MAR 1962 in Trinity, Los Angeles Co., CA, buried: 1962 in Trinity, Los Angeles Co., CA.

         d. Benjamin Otis CANNON, b. 31 JUL 1888 in TX. He married Ila Rebecca ROBINSON, married 1913, d. 20 MAR 1979 in Navarro Co., TX, buried: 1979 in Navarro Co., TX. Benjamin died 07 AUG 1977 in Hill Co., TX, buried: 1977 in Dawson, Navarro Co., TX.

         e. John Robert CANNON, b. 13 JAN 1891 in Italy, Ellis Co., TX. He married (1) Bernice KIRK. He married (2) Melvina STRANGE. He married (3) Gladys Lillian BURNS. John died 28 DEC 1960 in Temple, Bell Co., TX, buried: 1960 in Italy, Ellis Co., TX.

         f. Marjorie Katherine "Margie" CANNON, b. 12 JAN 1906 in Italy, Ellis Co., TX. She married Emmett Rogers BRACKEN, married 05 JUN 1921 in Ellis Co., TX, b. 18 JAN 1894, d. 04 NOV 1984 in Corsicana, Navarro Co., TX, buried: 1984 in Corsicana, Navarro Co., TX. Marjorie died 08 FEB 1975 in Corsicana, Navarro Co., TX, buried: 1975 in Corsicana, Navarro Co., TX.

2. Frank CANNON, b. 1854 in TX, d. 1860/9 in TX.

3. John Richard CANNON, b. 23 JAN 1856 in Gilmer, Upshur Co., TX. He married Joan DANIEL, married 17 NOV 1888 in Waxahachie, Ellis Co., TX, b. 28 JAN 1868 in Van Zandt Co., TX, (daughter of Jonathan DANIEL, Sr. and Artie Elizabeth EVANS) d. 22 APR 1917 in Italy, Ellis Co., TX, buried: 1917 in Italy, Ellis Co., TX. John died 06 SEP 1941 in Carrollton, Dallas Co., TX, buried: 1941 in Italy, Ellis Co., TX.

    a. Mary Lucy CANNON, b. 26 OCT 1889 in Derr's Chapel, Ellis Co., TX, d. 04 NOV 1889 in Italy, Ellis Co., TX, buried: 1889 in Italy, Ellis Co., TX.

    b. Joseph Franklin CANNON, Sr., b. 31 MAR 1891 in Italy, Ellis Co., TX. He married Ima Frances JONES, married 28 FEB 1913 in Italy, Ellis Co., TX, b. 12 JUN 1893 in Italy, Ellis Co., TX, d. 18 MAR 1977 in Balch Springs, Dallas Co., TX, buried: 1977 in Balch Springs, Dallas Co., TX. Joseph died 03 JAN 1968 in Balch Springs, Dallas Co., TX, buried: 1968 in Balch Springs, Dallas Co., TX.

    c. Pearl CANNON, b. 14 NOV 1894 in Italy, Ellis Co., TX. She married Russell Sterling WILLIAMS, Sr., married 05 AUG 1912 in Derr's Chapel, Ellis Co., TX, b. 22 APR 1897 in Moody, McLellan Co., TX, d. 29 MAR 1972 in Carrollton, Dallas Co., TX, buried: 1972 in Carrollton, Dallas Co., TX. Pearl died 13 APR 1951 in Carrollton, Dallas Co., TX, buried: 1951 in Carrollton, Dallas Co., TX.

    d. Richard Elva CANNON, b. 09 AUG 1897 in Italy, Ellis Co., TX. He married Helen Elizabeth MONTGOMERY, married 02 DEC 1941 in CA, b. 01 AUG 1904 in San Juan, Argentina, SOUTH AMERICA, d. 23 DEC 1988 in Paradise, Butte Co., CA, buried: 1988 in Paradise, Butte Co., CA. Richard died 13 FEB 1977 in Paradise, Butte Co., CA, buried: 1977 in Paradise, Butte Co., CA.

    e. Willie Inez CANNON, b. 04 OCT 1901 in Derr's Chapel, Ellis Co., TX. She married (1) Sam Jasper WILLIAMS, married 10 APR 1922 in Nacogdoches Co., TX, b. 1895 in Jacksonville, Cherokee Co., TX, d. ? in CA. She married (2) Robert Lee MAYO, married 14 OCT 1933 in Waxahachie, Ellis Co., TX, b. 29 SEP 1878 in Bath Springs, Decatur Co., TN, (son of James Benjamin MAYO and Martha J. BUCHANAN) d. 08 JUL 1942 in Italy, Ellis Co., TX, buried: 10 JUL 1942 in Italy, Ellis Co., TX. Willie died 01 MAR 1999 in Norwalk, Los Angeles Co., CA, buried: 1999 in Whittier, Los Angeles Co., CA.

    f. William Earnest CANNON, b. 18 FEB 1905 in Derr's Chapel, Ellis Co., TX. He married Velma Ione VAUGHAN, married 03 OCT 1928 in Waxahachie, Ellis Co., TX, b. 16 JAN 1909 in Florence, Williamson Co., TX, (daughter of James Richard Monroe VAUGHAN and Mable Clara MANTOOTH) d. 31 DEC 1995 in Lancaster, Dallas Co., TX, buried: 02 JAN 1996 in Waxahachie, Ellis Co., TX. William died 17 FEB 1966 in Italy, Ellis Co., TX, buried: 1966 in Waxahachie, Ellis Co., TX.

    g. Little Son CANNON, b. 08 DEC 1907 in Derr's Chapel, Ellis Co., TX, d. 12 DEC 1907 in Italy, Ellis Co., TX, buried: 1907 in Italy, Ellis Co., TX.

    h. Jewell Evelyn CANNON, b. 11 APR 1910 in Italy, Ellis Co., TX. She married Marcus Eugene "Buddy" BARNES, married 18 AUG 1928, b. 24 JUL 1897 in Paris, Lamar Co., TX, d. 01 OCT 1957 in Ft. Worth, Tarrant Co., TX, buried: 1957 in Ft. Worth, Tarrant Co., TX. Jewell died 15 SEP 2002 in Ft. Worth, Tarrant Co., TX, buried: 2002 in Laurel Land Mem Pk., Tarrant Co., TX.

C. Nancy Jane CANNON, b. 1838 in Maury Co., TN. She married I. R. GARRETT, married 17 FEB 1880 in Harrison Co., TX. Nancy died ?.

D. Syntha L. CANNON, b. 1840 in Harrison Co., TX, d. ?.

E. Caroline M. CANNON, b. 1843 in Harrison Co., TX. She married Dan CLARK, married 10 JUN 1884 in Harrison Co., TX. Caroline died ?.

F. Winney H. CANNON, b. 1846 in Harrison Co., TX. She married H. Mack SMITHSON, married 10 DEC 1861 in Harrison Co., TX, b. 14 MAY 1839 in AL, d. ? in TX. Winney died BEF 1880 in TX.

    1. Luvenia SMITHSON, b. 1863 in TX, d. ?.

    2. Van Hawton SMITHSON, b. 1865 in TX, d. ?.

    3. Attillar SMITHSON, b. 1868 in TX, d. ?.

III. Lucy CANNON, b. 03 SEP 1798 in Wilkes Co., GA. She married William THOMAS, married 07 OCT 1828 in Maury Co., TN, b. 1797 in KY, (son of Richard THOMAS and Mary "Polly" DAWSON) d. BEF 1860 in Harrison Co., TX, buried: BEF 1860 in Harrison Co., TX. Lucy died 00 NOV 1847 in Harrison Co., TX, buried: 1843 in Harrison Co., TX.

A. Joseph F. THOMAS, b. 1829 in Monroe Co., MS.

B. Mary H. THOMAS, b. 09 JAN 1833 in Maury Co., TN. She married (1) John S. CANNON, married 02 JAN 1851 in Harrison Co., TX, b. 1830 in Maury Co., TN, (son of Henry B. CANNON and Anna RICHARDSON) d. 1860 in TX. She married (2) *Unknown MITCHELL, married AFT 1860. Mary died 22 FEB 1896 in Italy, Ellis Co., TX, buried: 1896 in Italy, Ellis Co., TX.

     1.   (see children above),

    C. Louisa Jane THOMAS, b. 1834 in Maury Co., TN. She married Benjamin F. WILLIAMS, married in TX, b. 1828, d. ?. Louisa died ?.

    D. John R. THOMAS, b. 1836 in Maury Co., TN.

    E. Martha A. THOMAS, b. 1838 in Harrison Co., TX.

    F. William H. THOMAS, b. 1840 in Harrison Co., TX, d. BEF 27 Aug 1857 in Harrison Co., TX.

IV. Richardson William CANNON, Dr., b. 04 AUG 1801 in Wilkes Co., GA. He married (1) Elizabeth P. HUGHES, married 13 JAN 1823 in Maury Co., TN, b. 1799 in SC, d. BEF 6 Nov 1866 in Hempstead Co., AR, buried: 1866 in Hempstead Co., AR. He married (2) Anna MURPHY, married 06 NOV 1866 in Hempstead Co., AR, b. 1823, d. ?. Richardson died BEF 10 SEP 1870 in AR, buried: 1870 in AR.

    A. Elizabeth Porter CANNON, (daughter of Richardson William CANNON, Dr. and Elizabeth P. HUGHES) b. 09 MAR 1834 in TN, d. 30 APR 1910 in AR.

    B. Martha Rosanna CANNON, (daughter of Richardson William CANNON, Dr. and Elizabeth P. HUGHES) b. 1841.

V. Winifred CANNON, b. 13 JUL 1803 in Wilkes Co., GA. She married Richard A. HEWITT, married 24 JAN 1830 in TN, b. 29 DEC 1785 in SC, d. 16 NOV 1845 in Maury Co., TN. Winifred died 04 JUL 1878 in Giles Co., TN.

    A. John M. HEWITT, b. 05 NOV 1830 in Maury Co., TN.

    B. Robert A. HEWITT, b. 20 MAY 1832 in Maury Co., TN, d. 20 MAR 1890 in Union City, Obion Co., TN, buried: 1890 in Antioch Cemetery, Obion Co., TN.

    C. Marques D. Layfayette HEWITT, b. 21 SEP 1834 in Maury Co., TN.

    D. Martha J. HEWITT, b. 28 FEB 1837 in Maury Co., TN.

    E. Mary H. Cannon HEWITT, b. 07 APR 1839 in Maury Co., TN.

VI. Louisa CANNON, b. 1805 in Wilkes Co., GA. She married John W. MOORE, married 16 MAR 1839 in Maury Co., TN. Louisa died BEF 24 Sep 1867 in TN.

Looking for information on parents of John Cannon. Here are the facts on John:
1. John married Hannah ??? who says she was born in SC. Marriage would have been ca 1792 in GA or SC.
2. In 1795, he witnessed the purchase of land by Lucy Cannon in Wilkes Co. GA. Also witnessing this transaction was John Richardson. Both Johns are my 3GGF.
3. John and Hannah had 6 Children: Lucy Cannon b. ca 1793 (m. Thomas), Sophia b. ca 1795 (m. John Faris and William T. Aubry), Henry B. b. ca 1797 (m. Anna Richardson dau of John Richardson), Richardson W. b. ca 1799 (married Elizabeth Hughes), Levisa or Lovisa b. ca 1803 (m. John Moore), and Winney b. ca 1805 (m. Richard Hewitt). All children were born in Wilkes Co and married in Maury Co., TN.
4. John bought and sold land along Newberry Creek in Wilkes Co and was listed in the Tax Rolls for Wilkes Co. He lived close to the Richardsons. Other Cannons in this area were Pugh Cannon, Howard Cannon, Horatio Cannon, and Simcock Cannon. No relationship has been proven between these men. In 1797, Howard and Horatio witnessed the sale of property by Henry Cannon in Winton Co., SC.
5. John moved his family to Maury Co., TN ca 1807 along with several other families. Making this journey were the following families: Richardsons, Willises, Mills, Gambles, Thorntons, Popes and the Pullens. These families all settled in an area south of Columbia near Stiversville.
6. John gave part of his land in Maury Co to the trustees of a new church, called New Ramie, to be built.
7. John died ca 1831 in either Maury Co. or Giles Co. His will was recorded in Giles Co.

It has been shown that the Richardsons came from Newberry Co., SC to Wilkes Co., GA. Because of the close relation of the Cannons and Richardsons, this is a promising place for my John to have been born. An interesting coincidence is that Pugh, John, Howard and Horatio all had daughters that they named Lucy.

Questions I would like to answer:
1. Where and when was John Cannon born and who were his parents:
2. Who is the Lucy Cannon that was buying land in Wilkes Co. in 1795? Is she John's mother?
3. What, if any, is the blood relationship between Pugh Cannon, Howard Cannon, Horatio Cannon, and my John Cannon? Could they be brothers? Cousins?

Any help to untangle this genealogical knot will be greatly appreciated. Now for a commercial!! Visit my web site at:
http://www.metronet.com/~jrc/

J. R. Cannon
jrc@metronet.com

John Cannon is listed in the Maury County tax dook for 1813as owning 93 acres on fountain creek.

Children of JOHN CANNON and HANNAH are:

2.   i.   LUCY[3] CANNON, b. Abt. 1793, Georgia; d. Nov 1843, Harrison Texas.
     ii. SOPHIA CANNON, b. Abt. 1795, Georgia; d. Aft. 1860; m. (1) JOHN FARRIS, 18 Jul 1849, Muary Co. Tennessee; m. (2) WILLIAM AUBRY, 18 Jan 1860, Maury Co. Tennessee.

          More About JOHN FARRIS and SOPHIA CANNON:
          Marriage: 18 Jul 1849, Muary Co. Tennessee

          More About WILLIAM AUBRY and SOPHIA CANNON:
          Marriage: 18 Jan 1860, Maury Co. Tennessee

3.   iii. HENRY B. CANNON, b. Abt. 1797, Georgia/Maury Co. Tenn.; d. Abt. 1860.
     iv. RICHARDSON W. CANNON, b. Abt. 1797, Georgia; d. 25 Oct 1870, Arizona/Arkansaw.
     v.   LOVICY CANNON, b. Abt. 1803, Georgia; m. JOHN W. MOORE, 16 Mar 1839, Maury Co. Tennessee.

          More About JOHN MOORE and LOVICY CANNON:
          Marriage: 16 Mar 1839, Maury Co. Tennessee

     vi. WINNEY CANNON, b. Abt. 1805, Georgia.

No. 2

2. LUCY[3] CANNON *(JOHN[2], THE JOHN CANNON - TENNESSEE TO TEXAS[1])* was born Abt. 1793 in Georgia, and died Nov 1843 in Harrison Texas. She married WILLIAM THOMAS 07 Oct 1828 in Maury Co. Tennessee. He was born Abt. 1793 in Georgia.

Notes for LUCY CANNON:
Lucy Cannon of Wilkes Co., GA. In 1795, Lucy bought 140 Acres of land.

More About WILLIAM THOMAS and LUCY CANNON:
Marriage: 07 Oct 1828, Maury Co. Tennessee

Children of LUCY CANNON and WILLIAM THOMAS are:

     i.   JOSEPH F.[4] THOMAS, b. Abt. 1829, MS.
4.   ii. MARY H. THOMAS, b. 09 Jan 1833, Tennessee; d. 22 Feb 1896, Italy, Ellis Co. Texas.
     iii. LOUISA J. THOMAS, b. Abt. 1834, Tennessee.
     iv. JOHN R. THOMAS, b. Abt. 1836, Tennessee.
     v.   MARTHA A. THOMAS, b. Abt. 1838, Texas.
     vi. W. H. THOMAS, b. Abt. 1840, Texas.

3. HENRY B.[3] CANNON *(JOHN[2], THE JOHN CANNON - TENNESSEE TO TEXAS[1])* was born Abt. 1797 in Georgia/Maury Co. Tenn., and died Abt. 1860. He married ANNA RICHARDSON 06 Apr 1823 in Maury Co. Tenn., daughter of JOHN RICHARDSON and SINTHA WILLIS.

More About HENRY CANNON and ANNA RICHARDSON:
Marriage: 06 Apr 1823, Maury Co. Tenn.

Children of HENRY CANNON and ANNA RICHARDSON are:

5.   i.   JOHN S.[4] CANNON, b. Abt. 1830, Tennessee; d. Abt. 1860, Texas.
     ii. SALLY L. CANNON, b. Abt. 1830, Tennessee; m. MARSHALL BRASSELL, 17 Apr 1852, Harrison Co. Texas.

          More About MARSHALL BRASSELL and SALLY CANNON:
          Marriage: 17 Apr 1852, Harrison Co. Texas

     iii. NANCY JANE CANNON, b. Abt. 1839, Tennessee; m. I. R. GARRETT, 17 Feb 1880, Houston Texas.

          More About I. GARRETT and NANCY CANNON:
          Marriage: 17 Feb 1880, Houston Texas

     iv. SYNTHA L. CANNON, b. Abt. 1840, Tennessee.

v. CAROLINE M. CANNON, b. Abt. 1843, Texas; m. DAN CLARK, 10 Jun 1884, Harrison Co. Texas.

More About DAN CLARK and CAROLINE CANNON:
Marriage: 10 Jun 1884, Harrison Co. Texas

vi. WINNEY H. CANNON, b. Abt. 1816, Texas; m. H. H. SMITHSON, 10 Dec 1861, Harrison Texas.

More About H. SMITHSON and WINNEY CANNON:
Marriage: 10 Dec 1861, Harrison Texas

No. 3

4. MARY H.[4] THOMAS *(LUCY[3] CANNON, JOHN[2], THE JOHN CANNON - TENNESSEE TO TEXAS[1])* was born 09 Jan 1833 in Tennessee, and died 22 Feb 1896 in Italy, Ellis Co. Texas. She married (1) JOHN S. CANNON 02 Jan 1851 in Harrison Co. Texas, son of HENRY CANNON and ANNA RICHARDSON. He was born Abt. 1830 in Tennessee, and died Abt. 1860 in Texas. She married (2) [?] MITCHELL Aft. 1860.

More About JOHN CANNON and MARY THOMAS:
Marriage: 02 Jan 1851, Harrison Co. Texas

More About [?] MITCHELL and MARY THOMAS:
Marriage: Aft. 1860

Children of MARY THOMAS and JOHN CANNON are:
6.   i. WILLIAM HENRY[5] CANNON, b. 12 Dec 1851, Texas; d. 27 Oct 1929, Ellis Co Texas.
        ii. FRANK CANNON, b. Abt. 1854, Texas; d. Aft. 1860, Texas.
       iii. JOHN RICHARD CANNON, b. 23 Jan 1856, Gilmer Upshar Co. Texas; d. 06 Sep 1941, Carollton Dallas Co Texas; m. DESCENDANT J.R. CANNON OF TEXAS

           Notes for JOHN RICHARD CANNON:
            J. R. CANNON, ANCESTORS:
                He married Peggy Jane PUTMAN, (details excluded).

           Parents

           2.   William Earnest CANNON, b. 18 FEB 1905 in Derr's Chapel, Ellis Co., TX, d. 17 FEB 1966 in Italy, Ellis Co., TX, buried: 1966 in Waxahachie, Ellis Co., TX. He married Velma Ione VAUGHAN, married 03 OCT 1928 in Waxahachie, Ellis Co., TX.

           3.   Velma Ione VAUGHAN, b. 16 JAN 1909 in Florence, Williamson Co., TX, d. 31 DEC 1995 in Lancaster, Dallas Co., TX, buried: 02 JAN 1996 in Waxahachie, Ellis Co., TX.

           Grand Parents

           4.   John Richard CANNON, b. 23 JAN 1856 in Gilmer, Upshur Co., TX, d. 06 SEP 1941 in Carrollton, Dallas Co., TX, buried: 1941 in Italy, Ellis Co., TX. He married Joan DANIEL, married 17 NOV 1888 in Waxahachie, Ellis Co., TX.

5. JOHN S.[4] CANNON *(HENRY B.[3], JOHN[2], THE JOHN CANNON - TENNESSEE TO TEXAS[1])* was born Abt. 1830 in Tennessee, and died Abt. 1860 in Texas. He married MARY H. THOMAS 02 Jan 1851 in Harrison Co. Texas, daughter of WILLIAM THOMAS and LUCY CANNON. She was born 09 Jan 1833 in Tennessee, and died 22 Feb 1896 in Italy, Ellis Co. Texas.

More About JOHN CANNON and MARY THOMAS:
Marriage: 02 Jan 1851, Harrison Co. Texas

Children are listed above under (4) Mary H. Thomas.

No. 4

6. WILLIAM HENRY[5] CANNON *(JOHN S.[4], HENRY B.[3], JOHN[2], THE JOHN CANNON - TENNESSEE TO TEXAS[1])* was born 12 Dec 1851 in Texas, and died 27 Oct 1929 in Ellis Co Texas. He married SARAH 'KATHERINE' KATE FORTUNE 16 Jul 1881 in Ellis Co. Texas.

More About WILLIAM CANNON and SARAH FORTUNE:
Marriage: 16 Jul 1881, Ellis Co. Texas

Children of WILLIAM CANNON and SARAH FORTUNE are:
        i. EUNICE[6] CANNON, b. Abt. 1883, TX; d. Abt. 1954, Dallas Co. TX.

ii.   RICHARD EDGAR CANNON, b. 18 Nov 1884, Italy Ellis Co Texas.
iii. WILLIAM HENRY CANNON, b. 01 Dec 1886, Texas; d. 17 Mar 1962, Los Angeles California.
iv.   BENJAMIN ELLIS CANNON, b. 31 Jul 1888, Texas; d. Aug 1977, Dawson Navarro Texas.
v.   JOHN ROBERT CANNON, b. 13 Jan 1891, Italy Ellis Co Texas; d. 28 Dec 1860, Temple Beall Co. Texas.
vi.   MAJORIE KATHERINE "MARGIE" CANNON, b. 12 Jan 1906, Italy Ellis Co. Texas; d. 08 Feb 1975, Corsicana Nvarro Texas.

Appendix NOTE:

I would like to thank JR CANNON for contacting me and letting me know this very vital information. A message will be posted on Ancestry.com; Genealogy.com; Rootsweb.com and the Mormon Website at Worldwide Web.

And, now the continued genealogy from the beginning of this book for the **John Cannon** in **GENERATION No. 1**; and his descendants will follow. This family line of CANNONs first settled in **Virginia**; then moved down to **North Carolina**, remaining for a short time in **South Carolina**; settling in **Bulloch Georgia**. Then later descendants moved further south down in **Georgia into Thomas, Colquitt, Brooks Counties** where most of this line remain today. Some Cannon family members moved down in Hamilton Florida. Most of the CANNON family in the southern state of Georgia and counties are buried at **Pleasantfhill Baptist Church, Berlin Georgia.**

Generation No. 2

2. JOHN[2] CANNON *(CANNON FAMILY[1] HISTORY)* was born 1642 in Arrd-1656 Barbadoes/Lived in Barbadoes until 1660; then LivdCharles City Co. VA to Henrico Co. VA, and died 1695 in Henrico Co. Virginia/WILL 2/1/1696-97. He married (1) MARY PARKER. She died 1686 in She was his 1st wife.. He married (2) "ESTHER" HESTER PLEDGE 1670 in Henrico Co. Virginia, daughter of JOHN PLEDGE. She was born 1664 in Charles City Co. Va to Henrico Co. Virginia, and died Bet. 1703 - 1769 in She was his 2nd wife..

Notes for JOHN CANNON:
THIS JOHN CANNON departed from his homeland.

John Cannon departing from London; his occupation was a COOPER; and destination of ship was Barbadoes; dated April 12, 1656. John Cannon was an Indentured Servant to Agent Henry Bamber - Bristol-Mariner for four years length which would make his service end in 1660..

John Cannon he first settled in Barbadoes arriving there in 1656 - he lived there as late as 1660; then deciding to travel further to the United States.USA. In Barbadoes he was a Planter.

John Cannon first settled in Charles Co. Virginia upon arriving in the USA. Later he moved his family down in Henrico County, Virginia where he remained until his death.
He married in Henrico Co. Virginia where all his children were born.

John Cannons WILL dated 2-1-1696; named his wife as Executor of the Will in Henrico County, Virginia; along with John Pledge, John Redford and Nichols Perkins.

More About JOHN CANNON:
Land: 20 Oct 1665, October 20, 1665 - John Cannon owned 80 acres in Charles City County Virginia - on Kittawan Creek on the back of Weynock Bounding as followeth running along David Jones head line.

More About JOHN CANNON and "ESTHER" PLEDGE:
Marriage: 1670, Henrico Co. Virginia

Children of JOHN CANNON and "ESTHER" PLEDGE are:
3.   i.   JOHN[3] CANNON, b. 01 Apr 1688, Henrico Co. VA British Colony; d. 1734, Will in Henrico VA British Colony.
          ii.   WILLIAM CANNON, b. Abt. 1673, Henrico Virginia; m. MARY CANNON; b. Abt. 1708.

              Notes for WILLIAM CANNON:
              William Cannon

There is another record in Virginia indicating that William CAnnon married Judith Woodson b. 1673; in Curles Henrico County, Virginia. [Is it possible that he was married twice? More research needs to be done on this.]

iii. JOSEPH CANNON, b. Bet. 1675 - 1696, Henrico Va.
iv. MARY CANNON, b. Bet. 1675 - 1695, Henrico VA.

Generation No. 3

3. JOHN[3] CANNON *(JOHN[2], CANNON FAMILY[1] HISTORY)* was born 01 Apr 1688 in Henrico Co. VA British Colony, and died 1734 in Will in Henrico VA British Colony. He married MARY PRICE Bet. 1709 - 1710 in Henrico Co. Virginia, daughter of JOHN PRICE and JANE PUGH. She was born 1689 in Henrico Virginia, and died 1745 in Henrico Co. Virginia.

Notes for JOHN CANNON:
WHERE THE CANNON FAMILY ORIGINATED FROM:

The name Cannon is distributed throughout most of Ireland's counties but is most apparent in the counties of Donegal, Leitrim and Mayo.

Ui Canannain was the ancestral name of the Cannons and TirConnel (all of Co. Donegal and part of County Derry) was the "Land of the Cannons".

By the early 1600's the name of Ui Canannain had been anglicised to O'Cannon. Further anglicisation took place during the Penal Laws in the late 1700's and early 1800's and the name in Co. Donegal became Cannon. However in the east of the county and in the neighbouring counties of Derry and Tyrone the name, being spelt phonetically, became Canning.

O'Cannon, Cannon, Cannan, Canon, Canning are anglicised versions of the name Ui Canannain.

The Cannons are descended from two of Ireland's most renowned Kings: Conn of the Hundred Battles and Niall of the Nine Hostages. The O'Cannons have been described as "Ancient Princes of TirConnel" and "Valiant Chiefs" However their 350 year dynasty in TirConnel ended around 1250.

In the mid-thirteen century Rory O'Cannon and his son Niall became the power point for Gaelic resurgence. This contained the seeds of Irish nationalism which prevented the English expansion into TirConnel.

The fame of the O'Cannon kings of TirConnel has become a permanent part of Irish history through the survival of a number of placenames and antiquities such as: Letterkenny the largest town in Donegal and derives it's name from the Gaelic "Leitir Canannain" which literally translates as the "Hillside of the Cannons".

Several other place-names are derived from the O'Cannons: Carowcannon (near Falcarragh)-Cannon's Point, Lough Canannan, Drum Cannon. The earliest known Cannon Kings include: Rory O'Cannon who was High King of Ireland and TirConnel in C748, Hugh O'Cannon the Son of Rory, King of TirConnel in C1154.

Cromwell invaded in 1640 and most of the unfortunate Irish people, including any Anglo Norman settlers, lost their land. Ulster in the north was seeded with Protestant Scottish and English families.

In the early 1800's there were some 200 families bearing the Cannon surname living in Co. Donegal. These were mainly small tenant farmers barely subsisting on the meagre potato patches allotted to them. In 1845 the great potato famine culminated in widespread poverty and starvation and a great exodus from Ireland began.

Considerable numbers of Irish emigrated to the Americas, Australia and Britain, joining the armada of ships which sailed from Derry, Belfast, Dublin & Cork - bound for the New World. . Within 50 years the population was reduced to less than half.

In the early 1900's there was little more than 20 families with the Cannon surname left in Ireland. In 1841 the total population of Donegal was 296,000 - this declined rapidly after 1844 to a low of around 110,000 in the early 1900's.

Family researchers have discovered remnants of one branch of the Cannon family who emanated from Carrowcannon and moved to Burt in the east of Donegal, to Australia, to Washington D.C., New York and other parts of the U.S.A. Yet another branch seemed to emanate from eastern Donegal, around Castruse, moved to Derry, Co. Tyrone, England, Scotland, New York and Whyalla in Australia. It is now believed that this branch originated in Fanad. Other Fanad Cannings have left the area and moved to Letterkenny and all parts of the world including New Zealand.

Cannon is also found to be an English name and was a canon or clergyman on the staff of a cathedral or important church. Sometimes the name is derived from the fact that the original bearer was the canon's servant.

The name Cannon is distributed throughout most of Ireland's counties but is most apparent in the counties of Donegal, Leitrim and Mayo.

Ui Canannain was the ancestral name of the Cannons and TirConnel (all of Co. Donegal and part of County Derry) was the "Land of the Cannons".

By the early 1600's the name of Ui Canannain had been anglicised to O'Cannon. Further anglicisation took place during the Penal Laws in the late 1700's and early 1800's and the name in Co. Donegal became Cannon. However in the east of the county and in the neighbouring counties of Derry and Tyrone the name, being spelt phonetically, became Canning.

O'Cannon, Cannon, Cannan, Canon, Canning are anglicised versions of the name Ui Canannain.

West of Ireland bearing the name: CANNON or any of it's derivatives such as:
Canning, O'Cannon, Cannan, Canon, UiCanannain or any other similar name.

The Cannons are descended from two of Ireland's most renowned Kings: Conn of the Hundred Battles and Niall of the Nine Hostages. The O'Cannons have been described as "Ancient Princes of TirConnel" and "Valiant Chiefs" However their 350 year dynasty in TirConnel ended around 1250.

In the mid-thirteen century Rory O'Cannon and his son Niall became the power point for Gaelic resurgence. This contained the seeds of Irish nationalism which prevented the English expansion into TirConnel.

The fame of the O'Cannon kings of TirConnel has become a permanent part of Irish history through the survival of a number of placenames and antiquities such as: Letterkenny the largest town in Donegal and derives it's name from the Gaelic "Leitir Canannain" which literally translates as the "Hillside of the Cannons".

Several other place-names are derived from the O'Cannons: Carowcannon (near Falcarragh)-Cannon's Point, Lough Canannan, Drum Cannon. The earliest known Cannon Kings include: Rory O'Cannon who was High King of Ireland and TirConnel in C748, Hugh O'Cannon the Son of Rory, King of TirConnel in C1154.

Cromwell invaded in 1640 and most of the unfortunate Irish people, including any Anglo Norman settlers, lost their land. Ulster in the north was seeded with Protestant Scottish and English families.

In the early 1800's there were some 200 families bearing the Cannon surname living in Co. Donegal. These were mainly small tenant farmers barely subsisting on the meagre potato patches allotted to them. In 1845 the great potato famine culminated in widespread poverty and starvation and a great exodus from Ireland began.

Considerable numbers of Irish emigrated to the Americas, Australia and Britain, joining the armada of ships which sailed from Derry, Belfast, Dublin & Cork - bound for the New World. . Within 50 years the population was reduced to less than half.

In the early 1900's there was little more than 20 families with the Cannon surname. In 1841 the total population of Donegal was 296,000 - this declined rapidly after 1844 to a low of around 110,000 in the early 1900's.

Family researchers have discovered remnants of one branch of the Cannon family who emanated from Carrowcannon and moved to Burt in the east of Donegal, to Australia, to Washington D.C., New York and other parts of the U.S.A. Yet another branch seemed to emanate from eastern Donegal, around Castruse, moved to Derry, Co. Tyrone, England, Scotland, New York and Whyalla in Australia. It is now believed that this branch originated in Fanad. Other Fanad Cannings have left the area and moved to Letterkenny and all parts of the world including New Zealand.

IRISH
While the Anglicized version of Irish names are familiar to most people all Irish names have a long and proud Gaelic heritage. The original Gaelic form of the name CANNON is O'Canian; from the word Cano; which means Wolf Cub.

First found in Tirconnel [as stated in information already] North Ireland where they hed a seat.
Early settlers to found in records to be:
Edward Cannon and Ann Cannon whoi settled in Virginia in 1646.
John Cannon who first settled in Bardadoes in 1660 and
Another John Cannon settled in Jamacia in 1716.

Other CANNONS who settled in the USA are listed as follows:
Alexander Cannon, Andrew Cannon, Anthony Cannon, Burney Cannon, Bernard Cannon, Bridget Cannon, Charles Cannon, Cornelius, Daniel Cannon, Dennis Cannon, Edward Cannon, Ennis Cannon, [as seen below in continental soldier records of Virginia]; George Cannon, Hugh Cannon, James Cannon, JOHN CANNON, Mannis, Cannon, and Michael Cannon. Neal Cannon. Owen Cannon, PAtrick Cannon, Philip CAnnon, Thomas Cannon, William Cannon and all these men settled in Pennsylvania, Pa before 1772 and 1886.

COMING TO USA

The Abigail, 1622 Voyages are listed at ship name on Ship List
1622 The Abigail, from London, arrived at Virginia
Canon, John . . . . . . -- Age 20 in Virginia Muster, January 22, 1624/5

ELLIS CANNON
SPARTANBURGH DISTRICT
PRIVATE
VIRGINIA CONTINENTAL LINE
$96.00 ANNUAL ALLOWANCE
$251.89 AMOUNT RECEIVED
FEBRUARY 18, 1830 PENSION STARTED
AGE 86 born 1747
DIED MARCH 20, 1833

HENRY CANNON
GREENVILLE DISTRICT
PRIVATE
VIRGINIA MILITIA
$33.33 ANNUAL ALLOWANCE
$99.99 AMOUNT RECEIVED
APRIL 17, 1834 PENSION STARTED
AGE 83 Born 1751

1704 RENT ROLL of VIRGINIA:
Edward Cannon - Princess Anne County, Virginia 1704- Eventualy settled in Maryland
JOHN CANNON, Henrico County, Virginia 1705
John Cannon, Warwick Co. Virginia 1704

More About JOHN CANNON:
Land: 17 Aug 1725, John Cannon owned 50 Acres in Henrico Co. Virginia on northside of JAMES
RIVER; adjoining the land of Obediah Smith, Colo. Birdie and Gilly.
Land deed: 01 Sep 1709, A Deed of John Pledge lists that his land is adjoing JOHN CANNONS on Four
Mile Creek. Henrico Co. Virginia
Rent Rolls: 1704, Henrico County Virginia John Cannon is listed.1705

More About JOHN CANNON and MARY PRICE:
Marriage: Bet. 1709 - 1710, Henrico Co. Virginia

Children of JOHN CANNON and MARY PRICE are:
4.   i.   JOHN III[4] CANNON, b. 1709, Born Surry Co. Virginia; d. Dec 1783, Will in Wake Co. North Carolina
                  dated July 26, 1778..
            ii.   MARY CANNON, b. Abt. 1708; m. WILLIAM CANNON; b. Abt. 1673, Henrico Virginia.

                  Notes for WILLIAM CANNON:
                  William Cannon

                        There is another record in Virginia indicating that William CAnnon married Judith Woodson b.
                  1673; in Curles Henrico County, Virginia. [Is it possible that he was married twice? More research
                  needs to be done on this.]

            iii. WILLIAM CANNON, b. 1709, Owned 400 Acres of land Albermartle Co. Virginia; d. John Cannon was
                  witness to land deed 11-15-1750; m. JUDITH WOODSON.
            iv.   ELIZABETH CANNON, b. Abt. 1711.
            v.   JANE CANNON, b. 1708.
            vi.   JUDITH CANNON, b. 1709.

Generation No. 4

4. JOHN III[4] CANNON *(JOHN[3], JOHN[2], CANNON FAMILY[1] HISTORY)* was born 1709 in Born Surry Co. Virginia, and died Dec 1783 in Will in Wake Co. North Carolina dated July 26, 1778.. He married MARY [SARY] in Married in North Carolina.. She was born 1708 in Virginia, and died 1733 in Goochland, Virginia.

Notes for JOHN III CANNON:
Tradition is that he was the father of Archibald Cannon Sr. The Will of John Cannon of Wake County, North CArolina dated July 25, 1778 identifies his wife as Sary Mary??? and one son Archer Cannon.

In this Will he leaves a portion of his estate to his son Archer, provides for his wife for her lifetime and then leaves the remainder of the estate to his son Archer. No other persons are mentioned in this Will which leads to the assumption that Archer was the only child surviving at this time.

Roster of Soldiers from North Carolina in the American Revolution age 234; shows Arch Cannon in Militia #1349; Newbern District and also John in Militia #1136 of the same district. This reference also shows a John Cannon in the State Troops #2247, Newbern District.

John Cannon III initially lived in Surry Co. Virginia where he was born 1709. He married his wife whose name is either Mary or [Sary} ???. She was born in Virginia. She died in Goochland, Virginia in 1733. And so, the children listed would not have been her children. John Cannon III would have had to remarried after he moved down to Wake Co. North Carolina. This was the first migration of the CANNON branch we are writing about in this family history and genealogy. His children were all listed as born in Pitt Co. North Carolina. SO this family had to had lived near the border of the county if not in Pitt Co. N. Carolina at the time. Remember, that doctors were a scarce commodity then and one would have had to travel to where the doctor was located which would explain why the children did not get born in Wake Co. North Carolina.

John Cannon's second wife's name is not know at this time. There is so much confusion with his wife's name anyway; some stating it was Mary; some stating it was Sary. The fact that he would have had to have two different wives now explains the name discrepancies everyone is having.

John CAnnon III then died in Wake Co. North Carolina.

More About JOHN CANNON and MARY [SARY]:
Marriage: Married in North Carolina.

Children of JOHN CANNON and MARY [SARY] are:
5.   i.   JOHN[5] CANNON, b. 1740, PA Rev Soldier; d. Guilford Medina Ohio/Mound Hill Cemetery.
6.   ii.   ARCHIBALD "ARCHER" (SR) CANNON, b. 1745, Born Pitt, N.C. /Land Grant/Irwin 5/1839; d. 01 May 1820, Rev. Soldier Bulloch Co. GA/Died Bulloch Co/Ga.
7.   iii. DEMPSEY CANNON, b. 1772, Pitt Co. N. Carolina; d. Bet. 1850 - 1860, Bulloch Co. Georgia.

Generation No. 5

5. JOHN[5] CANNON *(JOHN III[4], JOHN[3], JOHN[2], CANNON FAMILY[1] HISTORY)* was born 1740 in PA Rev Soldier, and died in Guilford Medina Ohio/Mound Hill Cemetery.

Notes for JOHN CANNON:
John Cannon

History of Seville Ohio, REvelutionary Soldier Marker on grave is on side of Isaac J. Cannon's grave and a Military Star with 1776 is in the Center. Mound Hill Cemetery.

Child of JOHN CANNON is:
> i.   JOHN[6] CANNON, b. 1776, PA; d. 03 Aug 1857, Roxand Eaton Co. MI.

6. ARCHIBALD "ARCHER" (SR)[5] CANNON *(JOHN III[4], JOHN[3], JOHN[2], CANNON FAMILY[1] HISTORY)* was born 1745 in Born Pitt, N.C. /Land Grant/Irwin 5/1839, and died 01 May 1820 in Rev. Soldier Bulloch Co. GA/Died Bulloch Co/Ga. He married MARY JORDAN in Married North Carolina, daughter of JAMES JORDAN and MARY GLOVER. She was born 1748 in Born Jamestown, Virginia moved to Edgecombe, North Carolina, and died Sep 1850 in Bulloch County Georgia/she was 102 years old in 1850 census..

Notes for ARCHIBALD "ARCHER" (SR) CANNON:
Archibald Cannon was born in Pitt County, North Carolina. His father was buried in Wake County, North Carolina. After his fathers death Archibald Cannon moved with his family down into Georgia. Archibald initially settled in Irwin Co. Ga. but later he lived in Bulloch County, Georgia where he died. All of the children were either born in North Carolina or South Carolina; depending on where the family was at the time of the child's birth and as said before this is probably where a doctor could be found to help deliver the baby.

Tt is tradition in the family that he was the son of John Cannon and Sary or [Mary]; of Wake County, North Carolina. His daddy was also a Revolutionary Soldier and served in the Militia. Archibald Cannon is found in North Carolina Census 1790 and 1800 found in South Carolina. Apparently Archibald Cannon and his family were found traveling in about the southern part of North Carolina, western part of South Carolina and Bulloch Co. Georgia during his lifetime.

Roster of Soldiers from North Carolina in the American Revolution, page 324 shows Arch Cannon in Militia #1349, Newbern District and John Cannon in Militia #1136 of the same district. This was his father or it could be possibly his son John if the dates coincide accurately but no dates found on the information in history book.

A document of North-Carolina, Newbern District, No. #1349 dated August 30, 1783 certifies that Arch Cannon of Dobbs County is allowed one pound for Militia Duty. There is unconfirmed information that he may have deserted one company due to inadequate arms but enlisted again evidently in another company.

1790 Census of North Carolina Wilmington District, Bladen Co. page 187 CENSUS
> Cannon, Archibald
> Males 16 and up [3] under 16 [3]
> Females all ages [4]

A land deed shows that Archibald Cannon bought 100 acres of land in Bladen County, North Carolina July 16, 1795.

1800 Census of Liberty Co. Marion District South Carolina.page 803 list him as follows: This had to be the time the family has left North Carolina and traveling south into South Carolina before going west into Georgia, Bulloch County.

Males under 10 [2]
10 to 16 [2]
16 to 26 [2]
45 and up [1]

Females under 10 [2]
10 to 16 [1]
45 and up [1]

He is not shown in 1810 Census but he most likely has left South Carolina and traveled towards Bulloch County, Georgia because the deed records and marriage of their daughter Mary find him in Bulloch Co. Georgia.

Archibald Cannon is found in Wake County, North Carolina in land deed dated January 1789, at public auction for 5 pds. 10 sh. a tract of l00 acres on the east side of Buffelow Swamp, sold as the property of ARCHIBALD CANNON to satisfy an execution obtained against him by William Bagwell. This adds to the validity of John CAnnon and Mary or [Sary} ? being his father as John Cannon was found living in Wake Co. North Carolina.

Archibald Cannon served 11-20-1809 and Ensign for the 48th District of Bulloch Co,.., Georgia. for the Georgia Militia. Copy of Will recorded in Bulloch County, Georgia, 1812 has Archibald Cannon Sr.'s listing his children and grandson's which was probated in 1820. There is Deed information on property he owned and they had eight children. Tradition is that there were ten children, but only eight have been documented.

Page 55-57. LAST WILL and TESTAMENT reads: Nov. 14, 1812; Probated May 1, 1820. Recorded May 4, 1820. WILL of ARCHIBALD CANNON, SR.
Named wife, Mary, Sons: John, Demcey, Thomas, ARCHIBALD, Redick; daughters: Mary, Martha, Sary and grandson John who lived with him. Exec. Simeon Driggors, David Goodman. Wit: Simeon Driggers, Jonas Driggors, David Goodman.

In Bulloch County, Georgia this Cannon family attended the LOWER LOTTS CREEK CHURCH so research needs to be done to locate the cemetery records of the church and the Cannon family members who are buried there will appear on the list.

In 1820 Census he is shown as Archibald Cannon Sr. Bulloch Co. Georgia.

Archibald Cannon Sr is also found on land deeds of David Horton who purchased land next to or adjoining his property. So Archibald's property was located next to David Horton Plantation. June 30, 1794; as stated in David's WILL.

SOME ADDITIONAL CANNON Family Research [note this information does not pertain to our line; I just wanted to include it in order that other researchers might find some connection possibly.]

FOUND INFORMATION on a RICHARD CANNON, Savannah, Georgia, pg 29 Derby Ward, Gardens Farm 62E Farms (5).

List of First Shipload of Georgia Settlers - Egment & Manuscripts (1683 - 1748) CHARITY was the name of the boat. "ANN" was the name of the ship which brought the first settlers for the original 13 colonies. They landed February 13, 1733 at the site now known as Savannah, Georgia.

RICHARD CANNON; calendar and carpenter, aged 36 with Mary, his wife, aged 33. His sons - Marmaduke, aged 9; James- aged 7 months; his daughter Clementine - aged 2 1/2 months; his Servant Mary Hicks.

Richard married 2nd Wife - who was the Widow of Daniel Preston (Name unknown). 10-24-1734. He received Lot 5 in Savannah, Ga. He died 5-27-1735.

Marmaduke Cannon; orphaned 5/15/1740 at 16 years of age. He was later adopted in Court Record on 3/1740-41 by Joseph Wardrobe of Savannah; Carpenter.

Children: Mary died 6/22/1733.
    Marmaduke; Became Servant to Thomas Causton.
    James; died on shipboard on way to Georgia 1 year old.

Archibald Cannon Sr. died in Bulloch Co. Georgia May 1, 1820. Archibald's wife, Mary died in Bulloch County Georgia and lived to 102 years of age died Sept 1850. Mary was born in Jamestown, Virginia in 1748.

More About ARCHIBALD "ARCHER" (SR) CANNON:
Burial: Will of 1812 Bulloch Co., Georgia

More About ARCHIBALD CANNON and MARY JORDAN:
Marriage: Married North Carolina

Children of ARCHIBALD CANNON and MARY JORDAN are:
8.   i.   THOMAS[6] CANNON, b. 1782, Born North Carolina.; d. Aft. 1820, Bulloch Co. Georgia.
9.   ii.   JOHN CANNON, b. Abt. 1770, Liberty Co Marion Co. South Carolina 1800 Census; d. Abt. 1831, Giles Co. Tennessee.
    iii.   MARTHA CANNON, b. Abt. 1790, North Carolina; d. 1880, Ga/Mortality Sch./Colquitt Co/GA./Pleasanthill Bapt Cem/Berlin-Colquitt Co. GA.eorgia.; m. JOHN GREEN(E), 21 Jan 1812, Bulloch Co., Ga. Marriage Licenses 1795-1875; b. Aft. 1785.

    More About JOHN GREEN(E) and MARTHA CANNON:
    Marriage: 21 Jan 1812, Bulloch Co., Ga. Marriage Licenses 1795-1875

10.   iv.   SARAH "SARY" B. CANNON, b. 03 Aug 1799, Liberty, South Carolina; d. 02 Jun 1886, Jasper, Hamilton Co. Florida.
11.   v.   REDDICK (REDDIE) CANNON, b. 1785, Born N. Carolina/Rec. land in the GA Land Lottery.; d. 27 Dec 1878, 1820 Bulloch Co., Ga. Cen. Hd- Family/Died in Peniel, Putnam, FLORIDA.
12.   vi.   ARCHIBALD (JR) CANNON, b. 1784, born N.C/1st rec. in 1809/Militia Officer/Bulloch Co., Ga.; d. Bet. 1850 - 1860, Last in 1850 Census; not in 1860 Census..
13.   vii.   DEMPSEY CANNON, b. 1792, Farmer from N.C. 1860 Bulloch Co., Ga. Census 68 yrs old; d. 1886, 1820 Bulloch Co/Ga. CenHead-Fam. Died in FLORIDA.
    viii.   MARY CRIBBS CANNON, b. 28 Feb 1812, North Carolina; d. 22 Jul 1883, Bulloch Co. Georgia; m. (1) JAMES DILLARD BURGESS; b. 1801, Born in S. Carolina; Dooly Co., then Thomas Co., Ga.; d. 22 Jul 1883, Buried Old Bethel Prim. Bapt. Church off Tallokas Rd Brooks Co.; m. (2) SAMUEL [SIMEON ?] DRIGGERS, 22 Sep 1808, Bulloch Co. Georgia; b. 1785, Bulooch Co. Georgia; d. Wit on Archibald Cannons LWill&Testa.

    Notes for JAMES DILLARD BURGESS:
    Dillard Burgess - 1801 - 1865 BROOKS County, Georgia
       Born 1801 and came to South Georgia from Kershaw County, South Carolina. His father is believed to be Samuel Josiah Burgess shown in Darlington County in the 1970 census of South Carolina.

       Dillard married Agens Aness Cannon in 1831. Her parents were Archibald Cannon, Jr. and Mary Cribbs Cannon. Agnes was born inGeorgia in February of 1812. Agnes and Dillard had eight children.
       Dillard is believed to be the brother of William, Robert and Stephen T., who settled in Dooly County, Georgia. Dillard and Agness are buried at old Bethel Primitive Baptist Church off of the Tallokas Road in northern Brooks County.

    More About SAMUEL DRIGGERS and MARY CANNON:
    Marriage: 22 Sep 1808, Bulloch Co. Georgia

ix.   ELIZABETH CANNON, b. 1801, North Carolina.

7. DEMPSEY[5] CANNON *(JOHN III[4], JOHN[3], JOHN[2], CANNON FAMILY[1] HISTORY)* was born 1772 in Pitt Co. N. Carolina, and died Bet. 1850 - 1860 in Bulloch Co. Georgia. He married REBECCA in Bulloch Co. Georgia. She was born 1782 in Born Georgia.

More About DEMPSEY CANNON:
Land: 1827, Dempsey won a pick in Land Lottery/Deloach's District Bulloch Co. Ga. PARCEL located in Carroll County Georgia.

More About DEMPSEY CANNON and REBECCA:
Marriage: Bulloch Co. Georgia

Children of DEMPSEY CANNON and REBECCA are:
      i.   HANNAH[6] CANNON, b. 1809, Bulloch Co. Ga..
     ii.   NANCY CANNON, b. Bet. 1813 - 1816.
    iii.   RHODA CANNON, b. Abt. 1815, Bulloch Co. Ga..
    iv.   JOHNATHAN R. CANNON, b. Abt. 1825, Bulloch Co. Ga..
     v.   WILLIAM A. CANNON, b. 04 Oct 1827, Bulloch Co. Ga.

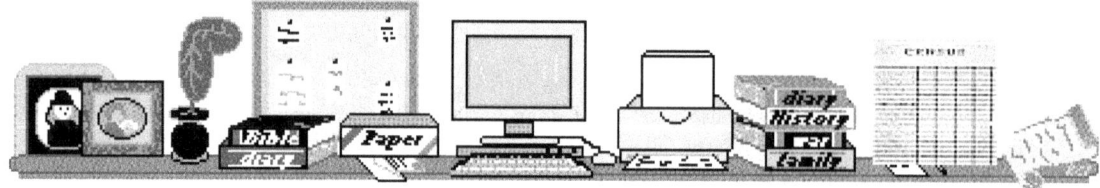

Generation No. 6

8. THOMAS[6] CANNON *(ARCHIBALD "ARCHER" (SR)[5], JOHN III[4], JOHN[3], JOHN[2], CANNON FAMILY[1] HISTORY)* was born 1782 in Born North Carolina., and died Aft. 1820 in Bulloch Co. Georgia.

Notes for THOMAS CANNON:
1820 Census of Bulloch Co., Ga.:

Cannon, Demsey

Cannon, Reddie

Cannon, Thomas

More About THOMAS CANNON:
Census: 1820, Bulloch Co. Head of FAmily

Child of THOMAS CANNON is:

14.	i.	MARGARET[7] CANNON, b. 1824, Georgia/1850 cen 26 yrs old/1860 cen 36 yrs old.

9. JOHN[6] CANNON *(ARCHIBALD "ARCHER" (SR)[5], JOHN III[4], JOHN[3], JOHN[2], CANNON FAMILY[1] HISTORY)* was born Abt. 1770 in Liberty Co Marion Co. South Carolina 1800 Census, and died Abt. 1831 in Giles Co. Tennessee. He married HANNAH in Giles Co. Tennessee.

More About JOHN CANNON and HANNAH:
Marriage: Giles Co. Tennessee

Children of JOHN CANNON and HANNAH are:

15.	i.	LUCY[7] CANNON, b. Abt. 1793, Georgia; d. Nov 1843, Harrison Texas.
	ii.	SOPHIA CANNON, b. Abt. 1795, Georgia; d. Aft. 1860; m. (1) JOHN FARRIS, 18 Jul 1849, Muary Co. Tennessee; m. (2) WILLIAM AUBRY, 18 Jan 1860, Maury Co. Tennessee.

More About JOHN FARRIS and SOPHIA CANNON:
Marriage: 18 Jul 1849, Muary Co. Tennessee

More About WILLIAM AUBRY and SOPHIA CANNON:
Marriage: 18 Jan 1860, Maury Co. Tennessee

16.	iii.	HENRY B. CANNON, b. Abt. 1797, Georgia; d. Abt. 1860.
	iv.	RICHARDSON W. CANNON, b. Abt. 1797, Georgia; d. 25 Oct 1870, Arizona.
	v.	LOVICY CANNON, b. Abt. 1803, Georgia; m. JOHN W. MOORE, 16 Mar 1839, Maury Co. Tennessee.

More About JOHN MOORE and LOVICY CANNON:
Marriage: 16 Mar 1839, Maury Co. Tennessee

	vi.	WINNEY CANNON, b. Abt. 1805, Georgia.

10. SARAH "SARY" B.[6] CANNON *(ARCHIBALD "ARCHER" (SR)[5], JOHN III[4], JOHN[3], JOHN[2], CANNON FAMILY[1] HISTORY)* was born 03 Aug 1799 in Liberty, South Carolina, and died 02 Jun 1886 in Jasper, Hamilton Co. Florida. She married COVINGTON "BRANICK" CRIBBS 13 Jan 1816 in Chatham Co. Ga., son of JOHN CRIBBS and JANE (?). He was born 01 Feb 1791 in Orangeburg, South Carolina, and died 16 Oct 1844 in 1844 Bryan Co. Ga./Wise Cemetery,Clyde Georgia.

Notes for SARAH "SARY" B. CANNON:
Sarah moved her family after the death of her husband because she lost the homestead. They moved to Sumpter Co. Georgia.around 1827.

Then Sarahmoved once more to Jasper, Hamilton County, Florida where she lived until her death.

Notes for COVINGTON "BRANICK" CRIBBS:
ID: I115980420
Name: Covington Brannick CRIBBS
Given Name: Covington Brannick
Surname: Cribbs
Sex: M
Birth: 1 Feb 1791 in Orangeburg, South Carolina
Death: 16 Oct 1844 in Bryan County, GA
Burial: Wise Cemetery, Clyde, Georgia
Change Date: 1 Oct 2000

Father: John CRIBBS
Mother: Jane ???

Marriage 1 Sarah B. CANNON b: 3 Aug 1799 in Liberty County, South Carolina
Married: 13 Jan 1816 in Chatham County, GA
Note: _UIDA910A7980A31BF43B364670D2A08E0B88AF5
Children
 Thomas CRIBBS b: 22 Oct 1816 in Georgia
 Archibald Brannick CRIBBS b: 3 Dec 1817 in Liberty County, GA
 Reddick CRIBBS b: 9 Jan 1820 in Georgia
 Mary CRIBBS b: 17 Dec 1821 in Georgia
 Jonathon CRIBBS b: 24 Jul 1823 in Georgia
 John CRIBBS b: 25 Nov 1824 in Bulloch County, GA
 Solomon Brannick CRIBBS b: 23 Jan 1827 in Georgia
 Covington James CRIBBS b: 9 Oct 1829 in Bulloch County, GA
 Sarah CRIBBS b: 24 Dec 1831 in Georgia
 Jordan CRIBBS b: 18 Oct 1833 in Georgia
 Martha CRIBBS b: 26 Jan 1836 in Georgia
 Owen Brannick CRIBBS b: 5 Apr 1839 in Bulloch County, GA
 Darrell Jefferson CRIBBS b: 8 Feb 1842 in Georgia

1.   Coventon cRibbs - found in 1820 Census of Bulloch Co. Ga. in the same area as Thomas, Dempsey and Redic Cannon who are all brothers of Archibald Cannon Jr. and John Green that married MArtha, a sister of Archibald Cannon Jr. This census shows his age between 26 and 45, lists 3 males under 10, 1 female under 10 and 2 females between 16 and 26.

2.   Covington Cribs - shown as JUSTICE OF PEACE in Bulloch Co. Ga. in the early 1800's.

3.   Elizabeth Cribb is shown as marrying Willie Newman on January 7, 1819 in Bulloch Co. Ga. in the same source Georgia Genealogical Source Material by Alvaretta Kenan Register. The fact that her marriage was only 8 years after that of Mary makes it possible that their ages were near the same and that they could have been sisters.

4.   Thomas Cribbs is shown marrying Eliza Smith December 5, 1839 in Bulloch Co. Ga.

5.   Archibald Cribbs is shown as being issued a license to marry Cloah Futch on April 3, 1841 Buloloch Co. Ga.

6. Redic Cannon is shown on a list of membership of Lower Lotts Creek Church in March 1833 and is further shown as being dismissed by letter. He is also shown as marrying Susan Wise on November 13, 1842 in Bulloch County. Marriage record shows name as Reddick Cribbs.

Covington was located in Bulloch County Georgia with his family in 1820.

In 1840 hemoved his family to Bryan County, GEorgia as can be seen in census records there.

More About COVINGTON CRIBBS and SARAH CANNON:
Marriage: 13 Jan 1816, Chatham Co. Ga.

Children of SARAH CANNON and COVINGTON CRIBBS are:
17.   i.   MARY[7] CRIBBS, b. 17 Dec 1821, Born in Ga.a pr cen./possibly [Bulloch Co.???]; d. Abt. 1925, No rec's after that cen.
    ii.   THOMAS CRIBBS, b. 22 Oct 1816, Born Bulloch Co. Georgia; m. ELIZABETH SMITH, 05 Dec 1839, Married Bulloch Co. Georgia; b. Abt. 1816, Bulloch Co. Georgia.

        More About THOMAS CRIBBS and ELIZABETH SMITH:
        Marriage: 05 Dec 1839, Married Bulloch Co. Georgia

    iii.   ARCHIBALD BRANNICK CRIBBS, b. 03 Dec 1817, Bulloch Co. Ga; d. Abt. 1879, Bryan Co. Georgia; m. MARIA C. FUTCH; b. 03 Apr 1841, Bulloch Co. Georgia.
    iv.   REDDICK CRIBBS, b. 09 Jan 1820, Born in Bulloch Co. Georgia.
    v.   JONATHAN CRIBBS, b. 24 Jul 1823, Born in Bulloch Co. Georgia.
    vi.   JOHN CRIBBS, b. 25 Nov 1824, born Bulloch Co. Georgia; d. Aft. 1824; m. EMILY J. KIMMY, 05 May 1854, Sumpter Co. Georgia.

        More About JOHN CRIBBS and EMILY KIMMY:
        Marriage: 05 May 1854, Sumpter Co. Georgia

    vii.   SOLOMON BRANNICK CRIBBS, b. 23 Jan 1827, Born in Bulloch Co. Georgia; d. 28 Feb 1904.
    viii.   COVINGTON JAMES CRIBBS, b. 09 Oct 1829, Bulloch Co. Georgia; d. 29 Jun 1900.
    ix.   SARAH CRIBBS, b. 24 Dec 1831, Born in Bulloch Co. Georgia; d. 10 Sep 1852.
    x.   REV. JORDAN CRIBBS, b. 18 Oct 1833, Born in Bulloch Co. Georgia; d. 14 Aug 1917, Hamilton County Florida.
    xi.   MARTHA CRIBBS, b. 26 Jan 1836, Born in White Springs, Hamilton Co. Florida; m. SAMUEL EDWARD MOBLEY, 14 Aug 1859, Florida; b. 1836; d. Bet. 1862 - 1865, Died during Civil War..

        More About SAMUEL MOBLEY and MARTHA CRIBBS:
        Marriage: 14 Aug 1859, Florida

    xii.   OWEN BRANNICK CRIBBS, b. 05 Apr 1839, born Bulloch Co. Georgia; d. 26 Dec 1915, Hamilton Co. Florida.
    xiii.   DARRELL JEFFERSON CRIBBS, b. 08 Feb 1842, Born in Bulloch Co. Georgia; d. Hamilton Co. Florida.

11. REDDICK (REDDIE)[6] CANNON *(ARCHIBALD "ARCHER" (SR)[5], JOHN III[4], JOHN[3], JOHN[2], CANNON FAMILY[1] HISTORY)* was born 1785 in Born N. Carolina/Rec. land in the GA Land Lottery., and died 27 Dec 1878 in 1820 Bulloch Co., Ga. Cen. Hd- Family/Died in Peniel, Putnam, FLORIDA. He married MARY GREEN(E) 06 May 1812 in Bulloch Co., Ga. Marriage Licenses 1795-1875, daughter of JACOB GREENE and FRANCES ACRE. She was born Abt. 1792 in Bulloch Co. Georgia, and died 30 Dec 1878 in Died in Putnam Co. Florida.

Notes for REDDICK (REDDIE) CANNON:

1820 Census of Bulloch Co. Georgia.

Cannon, Demsey
Cannon, Reddie
Cannon, Thomas

More About REDDICK (REDDIE) CANNON:
CSA: Bet. Apr - 20 May 1865, Served/ CSA FLORIDA Co. B, 2d Cav.
Membership: Mar 1833, lower Lott Creek Church Bulloch Co. Ga. Letter of Dismissal

More About REDDICK CANNON and MARY GREEN(E):
Marriage: 06 May 1812, Bulloch Co., Ga. Marriage Licenses 1795-1875

Children of REDDICK CANNON and MARY GREEN(E) are:

18.   i.   ELISHA W.[7] CANNON, b. 03 Aug 1820, Georgia; d. 08 Feb 1871, Peniel Cemetery Putnam Co., Florida.
19.   ii.   MARY ANN CANNON, b. 10 Jan 1829, Bulloch Co. Georgia; d. 11 Feb 1893, Florida.
20.   iii.   JOHN J. [TWIN CANNON, b. 09 Feb 1833, Ware Co. Georgia; d. 10 Apr 1880, Peniel, Putnam Co. Florida/Peniel Cemetery.
21.   iv.   PETER [TWIN] REDIC CANNON, b. 09 Feb 1833, Ware Co. Georgia/1880 Cen. Palatka Co. Florida; d. 04 Aug 1890, Peniel Putnam Co., Florida/Peniel Cemetery.
        v.   JAMES CANNON, b. Abt. 1835, Florida; m. (1) REBECCA SMITH; b. 1854, Putnam, Florida; m. (2) HARRIETT SMITH; b. 1874, Putnam Co. Florida.
        vi.   SARAH CANNON, b. Abt. 1815; d. 30 Dec 1878, Florida; m. JOHN L. BECKS, 01 Jan 1832, Newsnansville, Alachua, Florida; d. Grave marker reads: Co. B 2 Fla Calvary.

           More About JOHN BECKS and SARAH CANNON:
           Marriage: 01 Jan 1832, Newsnansville, Alachua, Florida

        vii.   ELZIE W. CANNON, b. Abt. 1822, Georgia; d. Puniel, Putnam Co. Florida; m. NANCY CANNON; b. Georgia.
        viii.   JOSEPH CANNON, b. 02 Jan 1839, Peniel Putnam Co. Florida; d. 05 Dec 1881, Peniel Putnam Co. Florida.

12. ARCHIBALD (JR)[6] CANNON *(ARCHIBALD "ARCHER" (SR)[5], JOHN III[4], JOHN[3], JOHN[2], CANNON FAMILY[1] HISTORY)* was born 1784 in born N.C/1st rec. in 1809/Militia Officer/Bulloch Co., Ga., and died Bet. 1850 - 1860 in Last in 1850 Census; not in 1860 Census.. He married MARY CRIBBS 19 Jan 1811 in Bulloch County, Ga. married 1st Cousin., daughter of COVINGTON CRIBBS and SARAH CANNON. She was born 17 Dec 1821 in Born in Ga.a pr cen./possibly [Bulloch Co.???], and died Abt. 1925 in No rec's after that cen.

Notes for ARCHIBALD (JR) CANNON:
Archibald Cannon, Jr. and Mary Cribb had nine children. Archibald was found for the last time in the 1850 Census; not found in 1860 Census, Sumter County, Georgia. Mary Cribb Cannon was found in 1860 Census in the home of one of her sons, so he probably died sometime between 1850 and 1860 Census.

FOUND ARCHIBALD CANNON in Bulloch County, Georgia on the list of MILITIA OFFICERS:

     it reads: "ARCHIBALD CANNON   Ensign   Nov. 20, 1809   48th Regiment commissioned Nov. 20th, 1809 in Buloloch Co. Ga. Genealogical Source Material by Alvaretta Kenan Register. At that time Jr. would have been about 25 years old and Sr. would have been about 65 years old.

Newspapers in Bulloch Co., Ga. reads the following account: "Mrs. Cannon, aged 104 years at her death in Bulloch Co., Ga., wife of one of the earliest founders of the county." this lady was his mother, Mary.

CANNON, Archibald marr. CRIB, Mary 01/19/1811

CANNON, General marr. DELOATCH, Mary 10/29/1844
CANNON, Isaac marr. STONE, Mary 04/26/1820
CANNON, Jonathan marr. FUTCH, Mary 08/02/1847
CANNON, Radie marr. GREEN, Mary 05/06/1812
CANNON, William A. marr. RIMES, Margery 11/19/1849

1820 Land Lottery Buloloch Ga. received land.
Nov. 11, 1833, Book 5, pages 231 - 234 rec. April 1, 1837 Bulloch Co. Ga. Courthouse Archibald Cannon sold three portions of his land to Thomas Isham.

1830 Houston County, Georgia Census.
Archibald Cannon

Males under 5 [1]	Females under 5 [1]
5 - 10 [1]	5 - 10 [1]
10 - 15 [1]	10-15 [1]
50-60 [1]	30 - 40 [1]

1840 Census 884th Militia District, Sumter County, Georgia page 167:
Archibald Cannon

Males 10 and under 15 [2]	Females under 5 [1]
15 and under 20 [1]	40 and under 50 [1]
60 and under 70 [1]	

Total in household was six. Employed in Agricultural was 1 and cannot   read or write was 2.

1850 Census of 26th District Sumter Co. Georgia, page 342.
Both John C. Cannon and James M. Cannon [2 of his sons] are also located in the same district in the census.
    Archy Cannon age 66 yrs. Male Farmer Value of Real Estate $450 Place   of Birth North Carolina.
    Mary Cannon age 59, female born in North Carolina
    Caroline Cannon age 13 Female [name is also illegible] born Georgia

[NOTE: that the ages given in both the 1830 and 1840 censuses would have made his birth between 1770-1780; the actual age given in the 1850 census would make his year of birth in the year 1784.]

Other information reported and recorded at Bulloch County Courthouse, Georgia; Index to Land Deeds and Listed in Bulloch Co. Ga. wich could pertain to Jr. or Sr.:
1. Arch. Cannon to John Waters for $100, 200 acres of a 500 acre tract, January 20, 1818 recorded Nov. 5, 1818, book AAA, pages 382 and 383.
2. Archibald Cannon purchased 200 acres in Bulloch County for $200 from John Godlef Zitterour (Zeteronere) of the County of Effingham, February 14, 1809, recorded October 28, 1819, Book AAA, pages 409-411.

Archibald Cannon Jr. and his wife Mary Cribb had their children all born mostly in Bulloch Co. with the last of the children born in Houston Co. Georgia. It is not known yet where he is buried, more research to be done.

Notes for MARY CRIBBS:
[Note: Another researcher has that Mary Cribbs first married a Jesse DAvis and more research needs to be done in this area. Proof? Where?]

ID: I115980424

Name: Mary CRIBBS
Given Name: Mary
Surname: Cribbs
Sex: F
Birth: 17 Dec 1821 in Georgia
Change Date: 1 Oct 2000

Father: Covington Brannick CRIBBS b: 1 Feb 1791 in Orangeburg, South Carolina
Mother: Sarah B. CANNON b: 3 Aug 1799 in Liberty County, South Carolina

Mary Cribbs Cannon appears with Archibald through the 1850 Census. The last record of her at this time is in the 1860 Census of the 26th District of Sumter County, Georgia, page 503; where she is found living in home of her son Henry as follows:

1850 Census Sumter Co. Georgia 26th District
    Henry B. Cannon, age 33, male farmer Value of Real Estate $1000
       Value of Property $350
    Elizabeth Cannon wife age 25 female
    William Cannon age 3 male
    Ann Zady Cannon age 2 female
    Reuben Cannon age 3 months male
    Franklin Dee age 17 male FArm Laborer
    Mary Cannon, age 68 mother of Henry B. Cannon. female

More About MARY CRIBBS:
Res.: 1860, living in home of her son Henry B. Cannon. Sumter Co. Ga. 26th District,pg 503 66 yrs old in 1850 census.

More About ARCHIBALD CANNON and MARY CRIBBS:
Marriage: 19 Jan 1811, Bulloch County, Ga. married 1st Cousin.

Children of ARCHIBALD CANNON and MARY CRIBBS are:
22.   i.   DANIEL JAMES[7] CANNON, b. Georgia; d. Buried at Pleasanthill Baptist Church/Berlin, Ga..
23.   ii.   AGNES ANESS CANNON, b. 23 Dec 1802, Family record born in GA. Huxford states born Feb. 1812 (?); d. 26 Nov 1862, Buried Old Bethel Prim. Bapt. Church off Tallokas Rd Brooks Co..
    iii.   ALIPHARIE [ALPHERE] CANNON, b. 1814, Georgia [Aliphorus???].
24.   iv.   JOHN CALHOUN CANNON, b. 1816, Born Bulloch Co.Ga/Age based on Cen. Sumter CoGa1857.; d. Dist 26&27 Sumpter Co.GA in 1860 Cen..
    v.   HENRY CANNON, b. 1828, Georgia/1840 cen shows him 10-15 yrs - 1830 cen shows 1 male under 5;it was him; d. 1850 Cen in home of brother James M. Cannon.
25.   vi.   JAMES JASPER CANNON, b. 05 Mar 1847, Georgia; d. 05 Oct 1910, enlisted GA Prosperity Cem/Brooks CO. Ga..
    vii.   SARY CANNON, b. 1838, Georgia/Named after her g-g Grandmother..
26.   viii.   JAMES M. [JIMPSEY] CANNON, b. 14 Mar 1823, born Houston Co., Georgia; d. 02 Oct 1897, Prosperity Cem/Ione-Brooks Co. Ga..
27.   ix.   JANE CANNON, b. 1819, GA/ shn as 10-15 yr old in 1830 cen.

13. DEMPSEY[6] CANNON *(ARCHIBALD "ARCHER" (SR)[5], JOHN III[4], JOHN[3], JOHN[2], CANNON FAMILY[1] HISTORY)* was born 1792 in Farmer from N.C. 1860 Bulloch Co., Ga. Census 68 yrs old, and died 1886 in 1820 Bulloch Co/Ga. CenHead-Fam. Died in FLORIDA. He married REBECCA CANNON in Married Both were a Cannon.. She was born 1792 in 68 yrs old in 1860 Bulloch Co. Ga. Census.

Notes for DEMPSEY CANNON:
DEMPSEY CANNON ---

Also shown on the 1860 Colquitt Co., Ga. Census in his home is:

Mary Cannon who is 102 years old, born in North Carolina.

More About DEMPSEY CANNON:
Membership: Mar 1833, lower Lotts Creek Church Bulloch Co. Ga. [letter of dismissal]

More About DEMPSEY CANNON and REBECCA CANNON:
Marriage: Married Both were a Cannon.

Children of DEMPSEY CANNON and REBECCA CANNON are:
28. i. ZILPHIA[7] CANNON, b. 04 Jun 1830, Bulloch Co. Georgia.
29. ii. JOHNATHAN R. CANNON, b. Abt. 1819, Bulloch Co. Ga.; d. Bef. 1856, Bulloch Co. Ga..
   iii. RHODA CANNON, b. Abt. 1815, Bulloch Co. Georgia; m. WILEY J. LEWIS, 25 Jul 1834, Bulloch Co. Ga..

     More About WILEY LEWIS and RHODA CANNON:
     Marriage: 25 Jul 1834, Bulloch Co. Ga.

30. iv. WILLIAM A. CANNON, b. 10 Oct 1827, Bulloch Co. Georgia.
   v. GENERAL J. CANNON, b. Abt. 1823, Bulloch Co. Georgia; m. MARY FUTCH, 02 Aug 1844, Bulloch Co. Ga..

     More About GENERAL CANNON and MARY FUTCH:
     Marriage: 02 Aug 1844, Bulloch Co. Ga.

   vi. HARRIETT CANNON, b. Abt. 1820, Bulloch Co. Georgia.
31. vii. NANCY CANNON, b. Abt. 1813, Bulloch Co. Ga..
32. viii. CELITY ANN CANNON, b. Abt. 1812, Bulloch Co. Ga.; d. 12 May 1865, Vernon Parish, Lousiana.

Generation No. 7

14. MARGARET[7] CANNON *(THOMAS[6], ARCHIBALD "ARCHER" (SR)[5], JOHN III[4], JOHN[3], JOHN[2], CANNON FAMILY[1] HISTORY)* was born 1824 in Georgia/1850 cen 26 yrs old/1860 cen 36 yrs old. She married JOHN C. CANNON 08 Jun 1837 in Houston Co. GA./possible cousin to John???, son of ARCHIBALD CANNON and MARY CRIBBS. For more on Margaret Cannon ---see John C. Cannon information.

15. LUCY[7] CANNON *(JOHN[6], ARCHIBALD "ARCHER" (SR)[5], JOHN III[4], JOHN[3], JOHN[2], CANNON FAMILY[1] HISTORY)* was born Abt. 1793 in Georgia, and died Nov 1843 in Harrison Texas. She married WILLIAM THOMAS 07 Oct 1828 in Maury Co. Tennessee. He was born Abt. 1793 in Georgia.

More About WILLIAM THOMAS and LUCY CANNON:
Marriage: 07 Oct 1828, Maury Co. Tennessee

Children of LUCY CANNON and WILLIAM THOMAS are:
      i. JOSEPH F.[8] THOMAS, b. Abt. 1829, MS.
33.   ii. MARY H. THOMAS, b. 09 Jan 1833, Tennessee; d. 22 Feb 1896, Italy, Ellis Co. Texas.
     iii. LOUISA J. THOMAS, b. Abt. 1834, Tennessee.
     iv. JOHN R. THOMAS, b. Abt. 1836, Tennessee.
     v. MARTHA A. THOMAS, b. Abt. 1838, Texas.
     vi. W. H. THOMAS, b. Abt. 1840, Texas.

16. HENRY B.[7] CANNON *(JOHN[6], ARCHIBALD "ARCHER" (SR)[5], JOHN III[4], JOHN[3], JOHN[2], CANNON FAMILY[1] HISTORY)* was born Abt. 1797 in Georgia, and died Abt. 1860. He married ANNA RICHARDSON 06 Apr 1823 in Maury Co. Texas, daughter of JOHN RICHARDSON and SINTHA WILLIS.

More About HENRY CANNON and ANNA RICHARDSON:
Marriage: 06 Apr 1823, Maury Co. Texas

Children of HENRY CANNON and ANNA RICHARDSON are:
34.   i. JOHN S.[8] CANNON, b. Abt. 1830, Tennessee; d. Abt. 1860, Texas.
     ii. SALLY L. CANNON, b. Abt. 1830, Tennessee; m. MARSHALL BRASSELL, 17 Apr 1852, Harrison Co. Texas.

       More About MARSHALL BRASSELL and SALLY CANNON:
       Marriage: 17 Apr 1852, Harrison Co. Texas

     iii. NANCY JANE CANNON, b. Abt. 1839, Tennessee; m. I. R. GARRETT, 17 Feb 1880, Houston Texas.

       More About I. GARRETT and NANCY CANNON:
       Marriage: 17 Feb 1880, Houston Texas

     iv. SYNTHA L. CANNON, b. Abt. 1840, Tennessee.
     v. CAROLINE M. CANNON, b. Abt. 1843, Texas; m. DAN CLARK, 10 Jun 1884, Harrison Co. Texas.

       More About DAN CLARK and CAROLINE CANNON:
       Marriage: 10 Jun 1884, Harrison Co. Texas

     vi. WINNEY H. CANNON, b. Abt. 1816, Texas; m. H. H. SMITHSON, 10 Dec 1861, Harrison Texas.

       More About H. SMITHSON and WINNEY CANNON:
       Marriage: 10 Dec 1861, Harrison Texas

17. MARY[7] CRIBBS *(SARAH "SARY" B.[6] CANNON, ARCHIBALD "ARCHER" (SR)[5], JOHN III[4], JOHN[3], JOHN[2], CANNON FAMILY[1] HISTORY)* was born 17 Dec 1821 in Born in Ga.a pr cen./possibly [Bulloch Co.???], and died Abt. 1925 in No rec's after that cen. She married ARCHIBALD (JR) CANNON 19 Jan 1811 in

Bulloch County, Ga. married 1st Cousin., son of ARCHIBALD CANNON and MARY JORDAN. He was born 1784 in born N.C/1st rec. in 1809/Militia Officer/Bulloch Co., Ga., and died Bet. 1850 - 1860 in Last in 1850 Census; not in 1860 Census..

Notes for MARY CRIBBS:
[Note: Another researcher has that Mary Cribbs first married a Jesse DAvis and more research needs to be done in this area. Proof? Where?]

ID: I115980424
Name: Mary CRIBBS
Given Name: Mary
Surname: Cribbs
Sex: F
Birth: 17 Dec 1821 in Georgia
Change Date: 1 Oct 2000

Father: Covington Brannick CRIBBS b: 1 Feb 1791 in Orangeburg, South Carolina
Mother: Sarah B. CANNON b: 3 Aug 1799 in Liberty County, South Carolina

Mary Cribbs Cannon appears with Archibald through the 1850 Census. The last record of her at this time is in the 1860 Census of the 26th District of Sumter County, Georgia, page 503; where she is found living in home of her son Henry as follows:

1850 Census Sumter Co. Georgia 26th District
    Henry B. Cannon, age 33, male farmer Value of Real Estate $1000
        Value of Property $350
    Elizabeth Cannon wife age 25 female
    William Cannon age 3 male
    Ann Zady Cannon age 2 female
    Reuben Cannon age 3 months male
    Franklin Dee age 17 male FArm Laborer
    Mary Cannon, age 68 mother of Henry B. Cannon. female

More About MARY CRIBBS:
Res.: 1860, living in home of her son Henry B. Cannon. Sumter Co. Ga. 26th District,pg 503 66 yrs old in 1850 census.

Notes for ARCHIBALD (JR) CANNON:
Archibald Cannon, Jr. and Mary Cribb had nine children. Archibald was found for the last time in the 1850 Census; not found in 1860 Census, Sumter County, Georgia. Mary Cribb Cannon was found in 1860 Census in the home of one of her sons, so he probably died sometime between 1850 and 1860 Census.

FOUND ARCHIBALD CANNON in Bulloch County, Georgia on the list of MILITIA OFFICERS:

    it reads: "ARCHIBALD CANNON   Ensign Nov. 20, 1809   48th Regiment commissioned Nov. 20th, 1809 in Buloloch Co. Ga. Genealogical Source Material by Alvaretta Kenan Register. At that time Jr. would have been about 25 years old and Sr. would have been about 65 years old.

Newspapers in Bulloch Co., Ga. reads the following account: "Mrs. Cannon, aged 104 years at her death in Bulloch Co., Ga., wife of one of the earliest founders of the county." this lady was his mother, Mary.

CANNON, Archibald marr. CRIB, Mary 01/19/1811
CANNON, General marr. DELOATCH, Mary 10/29/1844
CANNON, Isaac marr. STONE, Mary 04/26/1820
CANNON, Jonathan marr. FUTCH, Mary 08/02/1847

CANNON, Radie marr. GREEN, Mary 05/06/1812
CANNON, William A. marr. RIMES, Margery 11/19/1849

1820 Land Lottery Buloloch Ga. received land.
Nov. 11, 1833, Book 5, pages 231 - 234 rec. April 1, 1837 Bulloch Co. Ga. Courthouse Archibald Cannon sold three portions of his land to Thomas Isham.

1830 Houston County, Georgia Census.
Archibald Cannon

Males under 5	[1]	Females under 5	[1]
5 - 10	[1]	5 - 10	[1]
10 - 15	[1]	10-15	[1]
50-60	[1]	30 - 40	[1]

1840 Census 884th Militia District, Sumter County, Georgia page 167:
Archibald Cannon

Males 10 and under 15	[2]	Females under 5	[1]
15 and under 20	[1]	40 and under 50	[1]
60 and under 70	[1]		

Total in household was six. Employed in Agricultural was 1 and cannot read or write was 2.

1850 Census of 26th District Sumter Co. Georgia, page 342.
Both John C. Cannon and James M. Cannon [2 of his sons] are also located in the same district in the census.

Archy Cannon age 66 yrs. Male Farmer Value of Real Estate $450 Place of Birth North Carolina.

Mary Cannon age 59, female born in North Carolina

Caroline Cannon age 13 Female [name is also illegible] born Georgia

[NOTE: that the ages given in both the 1830 and 1840 censuses would have made his birth between 1770-1780; the actual age given in the 1850 census would make his year of birth in the year 1784.]

Other information reported and recorded at Bulloch County Courthouse, Georgia; Index to Land Deeds and Listed in Bulloch Co. Ga. wich could pertain to Jr. or Sr.:
1.   Arch. Cannon to John Waters for $100, 200 acres of a 500 acre tract, January 20, 1818 recorded Nov. 5, 1818, book AAA, pages 382 and 383.
2.   Archibald Cannon purchased 200 acres in Bulloch County for $200 from John Godlef Zitterour (Zeteronere) of the County of Effingham, February 14, 1809, recorded October 28, 1819, Book AAA, pages 409-411.

Archibald Cannon Jr. and his wife Mary Cribb had their children all born mostly in Bulloch Co. with the last of the children born in Houston Co. Georgia. It is not known yet where he is buried, more research to be done.

More About ARCHIBALD CANNON and MARY CRIBBS:
Marriage: 19 Jan 1811, Bulloch County, Ga. married 1st Cousin.

Children are listed above under (12) Archibald (Jr) Cannon.

18. ELISHA W.[7] CANNON *(REDDICK (REDDIE)[6], ARCHIBALD "ARCHER" (SR)[5], JOHN III[4], JOHN[3], JOHN[2], CANNON FAMILY[1] HISTORY)* was born 03 Aug 1820 in Georgia, and died 08 Feb 1871 in Peniel Cemetery Putnam Co., Florida. He married (1) HONOR SMITH 19 Nov 1848 in Alachua Co. Florida. He married (2) SARAH SMITH 23 May 1850 in Putnam Co. Florida. She was born 10 Apr 1828, and died 20 May 1883 in Francis, Peniel Cemetery Putnam Co. Florida.

More About ELISHA CANNON and HONOR SMITH:
Marriage: 19 Nov 1848, Alachua Co. Florida

More About ELISHA CANNON and SARAH SMITH:
Marriage: 23 May 1850, Putnam Co. Florida

Children of ELISHA CANNON and SARAH SMITH are:

    i.   ADELIA [ARDELIEAIS[8] CANNON, b. 26 Dec 1850, Putname, Co. Florida Peniel; d. 05 May 1923, Peniel Cem/Putnam Co. Florida; m. JOSHUA P. MAY, 02 Feb 1871, Francis, Putnam Co. Florida.

        More About JOSHUA MAY and ADELIA CANNON:
        Marriage: 02 Feb 1871, Francis, Putnam Co. Florida

    ii.   HENRY A. CANNON, b. 02 Mar 1854, Francis Putnam Co. Fla; d. 28 Feb 1936, 2-30-1936 Putnam Co. Florida.
    iii.   JACOB WILLIAM L. CANNON, b. 20 May 1852, Putnam Co. Florida Francis; d. 27 Dec 1908, Putnam Co. Francis Florida; m. LUCRETIA (LUCINDA) SHERROUSE, 09 Dec 1880, Francis Putnam Co. Florida.

        More About JACOB CANNON and LUCRETIA SHERROUSE:
        Marriage: 09 Dec 1880, Francis Putnam Co. Florida

    iv.   MARY A. CANNON, b. Abt. 1855, Francis Putnam Co. Florida.
    v.   JOSEPH R. CANNON, b. 02 Jan 1859, Peniel Putnam Co. Florida; d. 05 Dec 1861, Peniel Putnam Co. Florida Cemetery.
    vi.   JEFFERSON MONTGOMERY CANNON, b. Abt. 1862, Peniel Putnam Co. Florida; d. Peniel Cem Peniel Putnam Co. Florida.
    vii.   ELISHA ARNOLD CANNON, b. 25 Nov 1865, Peniel Cem Peniel Putnam Co. Florida; d. 1934, Peniel Cem Putnam Co. Florida.
    viii.   SARAH E. CANNON, b. 1867, Peniel Putnam Co. Florida; d. Peniel Cemetery Putnam Co. Florida; m. WILLIAM H. (JR) WIGG, 25 Dec 1881.

        More About WILLIAM WIGG and SARAH CANNON:
        Marriage: 25 Dec 1881

    ix.   LEWIS K. CANNON, b. Abt. 1869, Putnam Co. Florida.

19. MARY ANN[7] CANNON *(REDDICK (REDDIE)[6], ARCHIBALD "ARCHER" (SR)[5], JOHN III[4], JOHN[3], JOHN[2], CANNON FAMILY[1] HISTORY)* was born 10 Jan 1829 in Bulloch Co. Georgia, and died 11 Feb 1893 in Florida. She married WILLIAM BRYANT OSTEEN 15 Jan 1844 in Married Nassau Co. Florida. He was born 17 Nov 1824 in Chatham Co. Georgia, and died 14 Feb 1900 in Florida.

More About WILLIAM OSTEEN and MARY CANNON:
Marriage: 15 Jan 1844, Married Nassau Co. Florida

Child of MARY CANNON and WILLIAM OSTEEN is:
    i.   POLLY ANN ODELL[8] OSTEEN, b. 22 Feb 1854.

20. JOHN J. [TWIN[7] CANNON *(REDDICK (REDDIE)[6], ARCHIBALD "ARCHER" (SR)[5], JOHN III[4], JOHN[3], JOHN[2], CANNON FAMILY[1] HISTORY)* was born 09 Feb 1833 in Ware Co. Georgia, and died 10 Apr 1880 in Peniel, Putnam Co. Florida/Peniel Cemetery. He married ELIZABETH JANE FENNELL GRAINGER 23 Dec 1858 in Putnam Co. Florida. She was born 17 Feb 1839 in South Carolina, and died 07 Apr 1898 in Putnam Co. Florida/Peniel Cemetery.

More About JOHN CANNON and ELIZABETH GRAINGER:
Marriage: 23 Dec 1858, Putnam Co. Florida

Children of JOHN CANNON and ELIZABETH GRAINGER are:
- i. JOHN R.[8] CANNON, b. Abt. 1868, Putnam Co. Florida.
- ii. CHARLES CANNON, b. Abt. 1874, Putnam Co. Florida.
- iii. MARY MOLLIE ANN CANNON, b. Abt. 1861, Putnam Co. Florida; m. JOHN M. GOODSON, 15 Jan 1880, Married Putnam Co. Florida.

  More About JOHN GOODSON and MARY CANNON:
  Marriage: 15 Jan 1880, Married Putnam Co. Florida

- iv. MAGGIE ISABEL CANNON, b. Abt. 1865, Putnam Co. Florida.
- v. VIRGINIA CANNON, b. Abt. 1870, Putnam Co. Florida.
- vi. WILLIAM A. CANNON, b. Abt. 1878, Putnam Co. Florida.

21. PETER [TWIN] REDIC[7] CANNON *(REDDICK (REDDIE)[6], ARCHIBALD "ARCHER" (SR)[5], JOHN III[4], JOHN[3], JOHN[2], CANNON FAMILY[1] HISTORY)* was born 09 Feb 1833 in Ware Co. Georgia/1880 Cen. Palatka Co. Florida, and died 04 Aug 1890 in Peniel Putnam Co., Florida/Peniel Cemetery. He married MARY A. PINNER 25 Dec 1856 in Peniel, Putnam Co. Florida. She was born 21 Aug 1839 in Florida, and died 25 Sep 1916 in Peniel Putnam Co. Florida/Peniel Cemetery.

More About PETER CANNON and MARY PINNER:
Marriage: 25 Dec 1856, Peniel, Putnam Co. Florida

Children of PETER CANNON and MARY PINNER are:
- i. EMILY[8] CANNON, b. 1858, Putnam Co. Florida; d. Abt. 1903, Putnam Co. Florida; m. SQUIRES, Abt. 1850, Married.

  More About SQUIRES and EMILY CANNON:
  Marriage: Abt. 1850, Married

- ii. MARY K. CANNON, b. 05 Apr 1859, Putnam Co. Florida; d. 08 Nov 1914, Peniel Cem/Putnam Co. Florida.
- iii. JACKSON CANNON, b. 1862.
- iv. ROSA LEE CANNON, b. 1864, Putnam Co. Florida; d. Aft. 1940, Putnam Co. Florida.
- v. AROVILLA CANNON, b. 1866.
- vi. ELIZABETH CANNON, b. 1867.
- vii. REDIC J. JR. CANNON, b. 02 Mar 1870, Peniel, Putnam Co. Florida/Peniel Cemetery; d. 13 Oct 1963, Peniel Cem/Putnam Co. Florida.
- viii. SALLA CANNON, b. 1870.
- ix. PETER REDDICK III CANNON, b. 02 Mar 1875, Putnam Co. Florida; d. 28 Sep 1956, Peniel Cem/Putnam Co. Florida.
- x. WILLIAM CANNON, b. 1875.
- xi. ROBY CANNON, b. 1877.
- xii. JEFFERSON B. CANNON, b. 10 Apr 1861, Putnam Co. Florida; d. 05 Feb 1878, Peniel Cem/Putnam Co. Florida.
- xiii. JEFFERSON MORGAN CANNON, b. 03 Sep 1862, Putnam Co. Florida.
- xiv. JOHNNY T. CANNON, b. 04 Jan 1877, Putnam Co. Florida; d. 15 Jan 1880, Putnam Co. Florida.
- xv. SUSANNA C. CANNON, b. Abt. 1880, Putnam Co. Florida; d. Abt. 1911.
- xvi. MARTHA C. CANNON, b. Abt. 1883, Putnam Co. Florida; d. Abt. 1952.
- xvii. CYRUS PINNER CANNON, b. Abt. 1886, Putnam Co. Florida.
- xviii. WILLIAM (BILL) CANNON, b. Abt. 1888, Putnam Co. Florida.

22. DANIEL JAMES[7] CANNON *(ARCHIBALD (JR)[6], ARCHIBALD "ARCHER" (SR)[5], JOHN III[4], JOHN[3], JOHN[2], CANNON FAMILY[1] HISTORY)* was born in Georgia, and died in Buried at Pleasanthill Baptist Church/Berlin, Ga..

Child of DANIEL JAMES CANNON is:
- i. ESSIE[8] CANNON, m. OTIS COOPER.

23. AGNES ANESS[7] CANNON *(ARCHIBALD (JR)[6], ARCHIBALD "ARCHER" (SR)[5], JOHN III[4], JOHN[3], JOHN[2], CANNON FAMILY[1] HISTORY)* was born 23 Dec 1802 in Family record born in GA. Huxford states born Feb. 1812 (?), and died 26 Nov 1862 in Buried Old Bethel Prim. Bapt. Church off Tallokas Rd Brooks Co.. She married JAMES DILLARD BURGESS 1831 in Brooks Co., Georgia, son of SAMUEL BURGESS and MARY. He was born 1801 in Born in S. Carolina; Dooly Co., then Thomas Co., Ga., and died 22 Jul 1883 in Buried Old Bethel Prim. Bapt. Church off Tallokas Rd Brooks Co..

Notes for AGNES ANESS CANNON:
Agnes Aness Cannon married Dillard Burgess.

the 1850 CENSUS of Brooks County, Georgia.
    Dillard Burgess age 49 born in SOuth Carolina.
    Agness 38 yrs born in Georgia
    William Wesley age 17 b. Ga.
    Mary Ann age 15 born in GA
    Samatha age 12 born in Georgia.

DEATH RECORD: 1880 Mortality
Brooks   CANNON, John M.   60   M   W   M   GA   GA   GA   F   JAN
Appoplexy   1

More About AGNES ANESS CANNON:
Death Information: 27 Jul 1883, Discrepancy in date of death.

Notes for JAMES DILLARD BURGESS:
Dillard Burgess - 1801 - 1865 BROOKS County, Georgia
    Born 1801 and came to South Georgia from Kershaw County, South Carolina. His father is believed to be Samuel Josiah Burgess shown in Darlington County in the 1970 census of South Carolina.

    Dillard married Agens Aness Cannon in 1831. Her parents were Archibald Cannon, Jr. and Mary Cribbs Cannon. Agnes was born inGeorgia in February of 1812. Agnes and Dillard had eight children.
    Dillard is believed to be the brother of William, Robert and Stephen T., who settled in Dooly County, Georgia. Dillard and Agness are buried at old Bethel Primitive Baptist Church off of the Tallokas Road in northern Brooks County.

More About JAMES BURGESS and AGNES CANNON:
Marriage: 1831, Brooks Co., Georgia

Children of AGNES CANNON and JAMES BURGESS are:
35.   i.   WILLIAM WESLEY[8] BURGESS, b. 1833, lived in Dooly Co. GA in 1850; d. 1910, 1880/Dry Lake Brooks, Co. Ga..
36.   ii.   MARY ANN ELIZABETH BURGESS, b. 23 Feb 1835, born in Dooly Co., Ga.; d. 17 May 1909, lived in Brooks Co., Ga. most of their lives..
          iii. SAMANTHA BURGESS, b. 1838; d. Became School Teacher and died early..
          iv.   JOHN [S OR T. BURGESS, b. 1841, fought in the Confederacy-Civil War.; m. MARY STENCIL, 1860.

                More About JOHN BURGESS and MARY STENCIL:
                Marriage: 1860

37.   v.   JAMES MADISON BURGESS, b. 16 Nov 1843, Born in Dooly Co., Ga. - Confederate States Army.; d. 14 Sep 1923, of Colquitt Co., PleasantHill Baptist Church Cem. Berlin Ga..
          vi.   STEPHEN G. BURGESS, b. 1847, born in Ga.; m. CATHERINE MCCALL; b. 1850.
          vii. ROBERT BURGESS, b. 1850; m. JARVIE HERNDON; b. 1852.
          viii. NANCY JANE BURGESS, b. 1853, Brooks County, Georgia; d. 1922, Georgia; m. JAMES THOMAS (TOM) GLASS, 12 Jan 1873, Thomas County Ga. Marriage Record Book H, pg 371; b. 03 Jun 1852,

See Notes./age 9 in 1860 Cen.Mitchell Co. Ga. Camilla; d. 13 Nov 1926, 74 yrs; 5 mos, 10 days.; Cook Co., Ga./Springfield Cemetery Cook Co Ga..

Notes for JAMES THOMAS (TOM) GLASS:
THOMAS GLASS - known as Tom Glass.

His death certificate indicates that Jane Sapp was his mother; and James Glass was his father.

Place of Burial; Nov. 14, 1926 - Hout Grave Yard - he was widowed at the time of his death and retired. His place of residence was near Arue.

More About JAMES GLASS and NANCY BURGESS:
Marriage: 12 Jan 1873, Thomas County Ga. Marriage Record Book H, pg 371

24. JOHN C.[9] CANNON *(ARCHIBALD (JR)[8], ARCHIBALD "ARCHER" (SR)[7], JOHN III[6], JOHN[5], JOHN[4], JOHN[3] KENNON, RICHARD[2] KENNEN, THE KENNON/CANNON FAMILY[1] HISTORY)* was born 1816 in [Calhoun???] Born Houston Co.Ga/Age based on Cen. Sumter CoGa1857., and died Aft. 1863 in Dist 26&27 Sumpter Co.GA in 1860 Cen.. He married MARGARET CANNON 08 Jun 1837 in Houston Co. GA./possible cousin to John???, daughter of THOMAS CANNON. She was born 1824 in Georgia/1850 cen 26 yrs old/1860 cen 36 yrs old, and died Aft. 1870 in 1870 Cen. In home of dau. Arminda Cannon..

Notes for JOHN C. CANNON:
John C. [is this Calhoun???] Cannon was born 1816 in Houston Co. Georgia and is found living in home of his mother Mary and father Archibald Cannon, Jr. as well as brother James M. Cannon in the 1830 Census of Houston Co. Georgia. John C. Cannon is again found in the 1840 Census and now lived in Sumpter Co. Georgia in the 884th District. He had a child born in the Americus, Sumpter Co. Georgia.

John was a Farmer, Planter as most the people were in those days in the agricultural, rural sections of the State of Georgia. These folks would have had to endure the major hardships of life. These families raised their own vegetables, and meats such as cow, or pigs. In many homes they raised cotton to use in clothing. Or in some cases long road trips in wagons had to be endured to bring supplies from distances to their homes.

Families tended to travel together and settle closely in areas to keep in touch with each other as only horses, walking or boat travel could be done. Families usually ended up living nearby water resources until deep wells could be dug for their water resources. The other important thing is that the pioneers of these counties were also still enduring the Indian troubles.

John C. Cannon's father's name was Archibald Cannon Jr. and mother's name was Mary. John's grandfather was Archibald Cannon SR. and grandmother Mary [Jordan] Cannon of Bulloch Co. Georgia. Archibald Cannon SR died sometime between the 1850 & 1860 census of Georgia as his wife Mary was living in the home of Dempsey Cannon in Bulloch County, Georgia. Mary lived to be 104 years old. The elder Archibald Cannon SR and family attended Lower Lotts Creek Church in Bulloch County, Georgia and are most likely buried in the cemetery. More research to prove is needed.

John C. Cannon and wife Margaret Cannon [daughter of Thomas Cannon] had a several children before she died. Two of their children were possible twins??? Anyway, both the babies would have been very close in age if not twins.

Also further research as to where they are buried? Will need to be done on this couple. A review of Lower Lotts Creek Church in Bulloch Co. Georgia of cemetery records needs to be done. Also check the 884th Sumpter District church cemeteries for burial. Also check in 26th District of Sumpter Co. GA for burial records.

===
==

JOHN C.4 CANNON (ARCHIBALD JR.3, ARCHIBALD SR.2, JOHN1) was born 1816 in Georgia, and died Unknown in Georgia. He married MARGARET CANNON June 8, 1837 in Houston, Georgia, daughter of THOMAS CANNON. She was born Unknown in Georgia, and died Unknown in Georgia.

Children are listed above under (8) Margaret Cannon.

MARGARET4 CANNON (THOMAS3, ARCHIBALD SR.2, JOHN1) was born Unknown in Georgia, and died Unknown in Georgia. She married JOHN C. CANNON June 8, 1837 in Houston, Georgia, son of ARCHIBALD CANNON and MARY CRIBBS. He was born 1816 in Georgia, and died Unknown in Georgia.

Children of MARGARET CANNON and JOHN CANNON are:
    i. CALVIN M.5 CANNON, b. 1840.
    ii. HENRY P. CANNON, b. 1844.
    iii.ARMINDA CANNON, b. 1845, Georgia; d. Unknown; m. ALEXANDER GLOVER, Unknown; b. 1835, Georgia; d. Unknown.
        Notes for ALEXANDER GLOVER:
1880 Census - Robinson, Colquitt, Georgia - Malissa and Median Cannon on Census as sisters to Arminda Glover.

    iv. PAULINDA CANNON, b. 1847.
    v. CHARLES DAVID CANNON, b. 1850; d. Unknown.
21. vi. REV. GEORGE WASHINGTON CANNON, b. 1854, Sumpter, Georgia; d. November 6, 1936, Berlin, Colquitt, Georgia.
    vii. MALISSA CANNON, b. 1863.
    viii. MEDIAN CANNON, b. 1863.

More About JOHN C. CANNON:
Census: 1860, John is not located in any census records after 1860.

Notes for MARGARET CANNON:
Apparently Arminda was left with the raising of the twins in the family as the mother is not found in the 1870 census records of the Brooks Co. Georgia.

MARGARET4 CANNON (THOMAS3, ARCHIBALD SR.2, JOHN1) was born in Georgia, and died in Georgia. She married JOHN C. CANNON June 8, 1837 in Houston, Georgia, son of ARCHIBALD CANNON and MARY CRIBBS. He was born 1816 in Georgia, and died Georgia.

More About JOHN CANNON and MARGARET CANNON:
Marriage: 08 Jun 1837, Houston Co. GA./possible cousin to John???

Children of JOHN CANNON and MARGARET CANNON are:
      i. CALVIN M.[10] CANNON, b. 1840, Georgia/11 yrs 1850 cen./20 yrs old in 1860; d. FARMER Laborer. Residence: 1860, Districts 26 and 27, Sumter, Georgia[1]
      ii. JOHNSON CANNON, b. 1842, Poss. Jackson???/in 1850 cen 8 yrs old..
      iii. HENRY P. CANNON, b. 1844, Georgia/1850 cen 6 yrs old/1860 16 yrs old FARMER.
      iv. ARMINDA CANNON, b. 1845, Georgia; m. ALEXANDER GLOVER; b. 1835, Born Colquitt Co. Georgia.
      v. MARGARET A. M. CANNON, b. 1847, 1850 Cen 3 yrs old/1860 cen 12 yrs old..
      vi. PAULINE CANNON, b. 1847, Sumpter Co. Georgia.
2.   vii. CHARLIE [CHARLES] DAVID CANNON, b. 01 Dec 1849, Sumpter Co. Georgia, USA.
      viii. CARRIE LAVINIA CANNON, b. 1853, Twin/see Marthania Cannon.
      ix. MARTHANIA CANNON, b. 1853, 1860 cen 7 yr old poss. TWIN to C. Lavina Cannon.
3.   x. GEORGE WASHINGTON [REV.] CANNON, b. Jul 1854, Born Sumpter Co. GA/3 yrs in 1857 cen/Cen.1860,Sumpter Co. Americus, Ga. READ NOTES ON HIM; d. 06 Nov 1936, Cherokee Co.GA/Murphee Comm/Hwy 319-bet-Thomasville/Moultire GA.. New Hope Freewill Babt.Ch..
      xi. MALISSA [TWIN] CANNON, b. 1863, Sumpter Co.Georgia; d. In home of Alexander Glover with sister Aminda. i 1870 census /18 yrs old.
      xii. MEDIAN [TWIN] CANNON, b. 1863, Sumpter Co. Georgia/ in 1870 census 18 years old.; d. In home of Alexander Glover with Arminda..

25. JAMES JASPER[7] CANNON *(ARCHIBALD (JR)[6], ARCHIBALD "ARCHER" (SR)[5], JOHN III[4], JOHN[3], JOHN[2], CANNON FAMILY[1] HISTORY)* was born 05 Mar 1847 in Georgia, and died 05 Oct 1910 in enlisted GA Prosperity Cem/Brooks CO. Ga.. He married (1) JULIA ELIZABETH SCOTT. He married (2) SARAH M. JORDAN. He married (3) MELISSA MERIDITH.

Notes for JAMES JASPER CANNON:
Julia married a Cannon. I have a Julia Elizabeth Scott
marrying James Jasper Cannon. Sorry cant help with dates yet. But I am working on that... Hope that helps you some.
Julia and James gave birth to my grandfather, Stephen Cannon. They all lived in Early County.

James Jasper Cannon served CSA - Clinch's Battery Georgia Light Artillery.
3/5/1847. Georgia.

More About JAMES JASPER CANNON:
Burial: Prosperity Cemetery

Child of JAMES CANNON and JULIA SCOTT is:
  i. STEPHEN[8] CANNON.

Children of JAMES CANNON and MELISSA MERIDITH are:
  ii. WILLIAM ARCHIBALD[8] CANNON, b. 30 May 1876, Georgia; d. 30 Apr 1938, Georgia.
  iii. JESSE CANNON.
  iv. JAMES ALLISON CANNON.

26. JAMES M. [JIMPSEY][7] CANNON *(ARCHIBALD (JR)[6], ARCHIBALD "ARCHER" (SR)[5], JOHN III[4], JOHN[3], JOHN[2], CANNON FAMILY[1] HISTORY)* was born 14 Mar 1823 in born Houston Co., Georgia, and died 02 Oct 1897 in Prosperity Cem/Ione-Brooks Co. Ga.. He married EMILY SARAH HOLLY. She was born 25 Oct 1826 in Georgia, and died 05 Oct 1911 in Prosperity Cem/Ione - Brooks Co. Georgia.

Children of JAMES CANNON and EMILY HOLLY are:
  i. JOSEPH A.[8] CANNON, b. 05 May 1847, Georgia; d. 05 Oct 1910, Georgia.
40. ii. DANIEL JAMES CANNON, b. 21 Oct 1848, Georgia; d. 22 Dec 1920, Colquitt Co. Ga..
41. iii. RANDALL ROAN CANNON, b. 05 Jan 1850, Sumpter Co. Ga.; d. 08 May 1929, Altha Calhoun Co. Ga./Pleasanthill BApt Colquitt Co GA Cem..
42. iv. ROXANNA ROSETTA CANNON, b. 1856.
43. v. SARAH SERNA CANNON, b. 30 Apr 1857, Georgia; d. 15 Apr 1936, Prosperity Cem/Ione,Brooks Co. Ga..
  vi. JAMES CANNON, b. 06 Apr 1861, Georgia; d. 30 Apr 1911, Georgia.
  vii. LETTIE ANN CANNON, b. 1868, Georgia; d. 1924, Georgia.
  viii. DOLLY CANNON.

27. JANE[7] CANNON *(ARCHIBALD (JR)[6], ARCHIBALD "ARCHER" (SR)[5], JOHN III[4], JOHN[3], JOHN[2], CANNON FAMILY[1] HISTORY)* was born 1819 in GA/ shn as 10-15 yr old in 1830 cen. She married LEWIS LAMP.

Children of JANE CANNON and LEWIS LAMP are:
  i. MARY ANN[8] LAMP, b. 1845.
44. ii. AMANDA JANE LAMP, b. 1852.
  iii. AARON LAMP.
  iv. JOHN LAMP.

28. ZILPHIA[7] CANNON *(DEMPSEY[6], ARCHIBALD "ARCHER" (SR)[5], JOHN III[4], JOHN[3], JOHN[2], CANNON FAMILY[1] HISTORY)* was born 04 Jun 1830 in Bulloch Co. Georgia. She married HENRY KENNEDY. He was born 1813 in 1880 Enum. Dist Tattnall Co. Georgia-FARMER.

Children of ZILPHIA CANNON and HENRY KENNEDY are:
  - i. LEVENIA[8] KENNEDY, b. 17 Feb 1863.
  - ii. JOHN G. KENNEDY, b. 04 Apr 1864.
  - iii. JAMES JASPER KENNEDY, b. 04 Apr 1867.

29. JOHNATHAN R.[7] CANNON *(DEMPSEY[6], ARCHIBALD "ARCHER" (SR)[5], JOHN III[4], JOHN[3], JOHN[2], CANNON FAMILY[1] HISTORY)* was born Abt. 1819 in Bulloch Co. Ga., and died Bef. 1856 in Bulloch Co. Ga.. He married MARY ANN FUTCH 08 Aug 1847 in Bulloch Co. Georgia, daughter of SOLOMON FUTCH and SARAH DAVIS. She was born 1829 in Bulloch Co. Georgia, and died in Bryan Co. Georgia.

More About JOHNATHAN CANNON and MARY FUTCH:
Marriage: 08 Aug 1847, Bulloch Co. Georgia

Children of JOHNATHAN CANNON and MARY FUTCH are:
| 45. | i. | SERENA[8] CANNON, b. 29 Sep 1848, Bulloch Georgia; d. 30 Aug 1881, Corinth Cemetery, Ft. Stewart, Ga. Bryan Co. Georgia. |
| 46. | ii. | JAMES WILIAM CANNON, b. 1851, Bryan Co. Georgia; d. 16 May 1909, 1880 Cen/Bryan Co. Ga.. |

30. WILLIAM A.[7] CANNON *(DEMPSEY[6], ARCHIBALD "ARCHER" (SR)[5], JOHN III[4], JOHN[3], JOHN[2], CANNON FAMILY[1] HISTORY)* was born 10 Oct 1827 in Bulloch Co. Georgia. He married MARGARET WISE in Bulloch Co. Georgia. She was born 11 Nov 1823 in Bulloch Co. Georgia, and died in Died in Bryan Co. Ga.Ellabell, Bryan Co., Georgia Smith-Bird Cemetary.

More About WILLIAM CANNON and MARGARET WISE:
Marriage: Bulloch Co. Georgia

Children of WILLIAM CANNON and MARGARET WISE are:
47.	i.	JOHN ROBERT[8] CANNON, b. Abt. 1848, Bulloch Co. Ga.; d. 04 Nov 1910, Bulloch Co. Ga..
	ii.	ADDIE CANNON, b. Abt. 1852.
48.	iii.	NATHAN A. CANNON, b. 27 Dec 1853, Bryan Co. Ga.; d. 02 May 1916, Bryan Co. Georgia.
	iv.	MATTHEW D. CANNON, b. Abt. 1856, Bulloch Co. Georgia; d. 11 Apr 1909; m. ARDELA VIRGINIA ROGERS; b. Abt. 1862; d. 25 Sep 1894, Bryan Co. Ga..
	v.	SARAH CANNON, b. Bet. 1856 - 1858, Bulloch Co. Georgia.
	vi.	REBECCA ADELINE CANNON, b. 24 Feb 1848, Bryan Co. Georgia; d. 01 May 1934, Ellabell, Bryan Co., Georgia Smith-Bird Cemetary.
	vii.	HENRY C. CANNON, b. Abt. 1861, Bulloch Co. Ga..
	viii.	MARGARET CANNON, b. Abt. 1863, Bryan Co. Georgia.
	ix.	JOSHUA OSCAR CANNON, b. 16 Oct 1860, Bryan Co. Ga..

31. NANCY[7] CANNON *(DEMPSEY[6], ARCHIBALD "ARCHER" (SR)[5], JOHN III[4], JOHN[3], JOHN[2], CANNON FAMILY[1] HISTORY)* was born Abt. 1813 in Bulloch Co. Ga.. She married ABRAHAM B. RIGGS 06 Nov 1834 in Bulloch Co. Ga.. He was born 1814 in Bulloch Co. Georgia.

More About ABRAHAM RIGGS and NANCY CANNON:
Marriage: 06 Nov 1834, Bulloch Co. Ga.

Child of NANCY CANNON and ABRAHAM RIGGS is:
  - i. HARMON[8] RIGGS, b. Abt. 1843, Bulloch Co. Georgia; m. ANN VIOLA LEE.

32. CELITY ANN[7] CANNON *(DEMPSEY[6], ARCHIBALD "ARCHER" (SR)[5], JOHN III[4], JOHN[3], JOHN[2], CANNON FAMILY[1] HISTORY)* was born Abt. 1812 in Bulloch Co. Ga., and died 12 May 1865 in Vernon Parish, Lousiana. She married ELANDER NESMITH 15 Mar 1830 in Bulloch Co. Georgia. He was born 17 Apr 1803 in Screven Co. Georgia, and died 15 Sep 1877 in Vernon Parish Louisiana.

More About ELANDER NESMITH and CELITY CANNON:
Marriage: 15 Mar 1830, Bulloch Co. Georgia

Children of CELITY CANNON and ELANDER NESMITH are:

   i.   AMANDA [TWIN][8] NESMITH, b. 18 Apr 1832, Bulloch Co. Georgia; d. 20 Dec 1876, Nachitachis Parish Louisiana.
   ii. MALACHI [TWIN] NESMITH, b. 19 Apr 1832, Bulloch Co. Georgia; d. 18 Apr 1863, Richmond Virginia Cvil War Casualty.
   iii. MARGARET ELIZABETH NESMITH, b. 01 May 1838, Thoms County Georgia; d. 20 Apr 1895, Vernon Parish Louisiana.
   iv. CHYLER NESMITH, b. 31 Jan 1838, Bulloch Co. Ga.; d. 26 Jan 1905, Natchitachis Parish Louisiana.
   v.   AUGUSTUS NESMITH, b. 29 Jan 1839, Bulloch Co. Georgia; d. 02 Jan 1863, Vicksburg, Miss. Civil War Casualty.
   vi. JOHN NESMITH, b. 07 Mar 1842, Thomas Co. Georgia; d. 20 May 1862, Clinton, Miss. Civil War Casualty.
   vii. REBECCA NESMITH, b. 19 Jan 1844, Thomas Co. Ga.; d. 14 Mar 1889, Vernon Parish Louisiana.
   viii. NANCY JANE NESMITH, b. 28 Mar 1846, Thomas Co. Ga.; d. 01 Feb 1927, leesville, Lousiana.
   ix. ELEANDER JR. NESMITH, b. 22 Apr 1848, Thomas Co. Ga.; d. 1878, Palastine Texas.

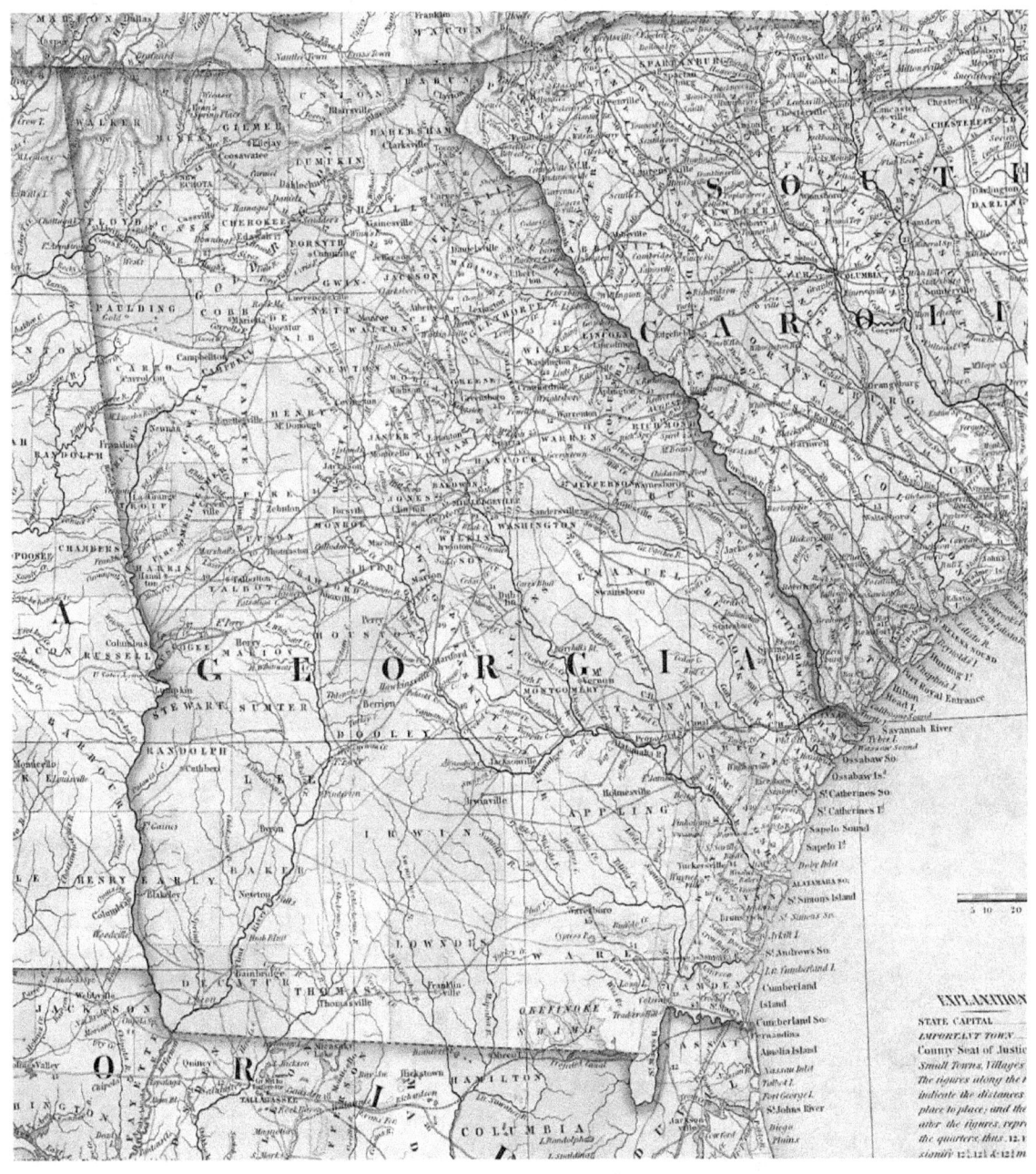

Generation No. 8

33. MARY H.[8] THOMAS *(LUCY[7] CANNON, JOHN[6], ARCHIBALD "ARCHER" (SR)[5], JOHN III[4], JOHN[3], JOHN[2], CANNON FAMILY[1] HISTORY)* was born 09 Jan 1833 in Tennessee, and died 22 Feb 1896 in Italy, Ellis Co. Texas. She married (1) JOHN S. CANNON 02 Jan 1851 in Harrison Co. Texas, son of HENRY CANNON and ANNA RICHARDSON. He was born Abt. 1830 in Tennessee, and died Abt. 1860 in Texas. She married (2) [?] MITCHELL Aft. 1860.

More About JOHN CANNON and MARY THOMAS:
Marriage: 02 Jan 1851, Harrison Co. Texas

More About [?] MITCHELL and MARY THOMAS:
Marriage: Aft. 1860

Children of MARY THOMAS and JOHN CANNON are:
49.   i.   WILLIAM HENRY[9] CANNON, b. 12 Dec 1851, Texas; d. 27 Oct 1929, Ellis Co Texas.
      ii.   FRANK CANNON, b. Abt. 1854, Texas; d. Aft. 1860, Texas.
     iii.   JOHN RICHARD CANNON, b. 23 Jan 1856, Gilmer Upshar Co. Texas; d. 06 Sep 1941, Carollton Dallas Co Texas.

34. JOHN S.[8] CANNON *(HENRY B.[7], JOHN[6], ARCHIBALD "ARCHER" (SR)[5], JOHN III[4], JOHN[3], JOHN[2], CANNON FAMILY[1] HISTORY)* was born Abt. 1830 in Tennessee, and died Abt. 1860 in Texas. He married MARY H. THOMAS 02 Jan 1851 in Harrison Co. Texas, daughter of WILLIAM THOMAS and LUCY CANNON. She was born 09 Jan 1833 in Tennessee, and died 22 Feb 1896 in Italy, Ellis Co. Texas.

More About JOHN CANNON and MARY THOMAS:
Marriage: 02 Jan 1851, Harrison Co. Texas

Children are listed above under (33) Mary H. Thomas.

35. WILLIAM WESLEY[8] BURGESS *(AGNES ANESS[7] CANNON, ARCHIBALD (JR)[6], ARCHIBALD "ARCHER" (SR)[5], JOHN III[4], JOHN[3], JOHN[2], CANNON FAMILY[1] HISTORY)* was born 1833 in lived in Dooly Co. GA in 1850, and died 1910 in 1880/Dry Lake Brooks, Co. Ga.. He married SUSAN BOONE in Lived in Dooly Co, Ga. in c 1850.. She was born 1837, and died 1902.

More About WILLIAM BURGESS and SUSAN BOONE:
Marriage: Lived in Dooly Co, Ga. in c 1850.

Children of WILLIAM BURGESS and SUSAN BOONE are:
      i.   WILLIAM T.[9] BURGESS, b. 1859.
     ii.   JAMES L. BURGESS, b. 1861.
    iii.   ROBERT H. BURGESS, b. 1869.
    iv.   LAURA L. BURGESS, b. 1873.
     v.   LUDIE L. BURGESS, b. 1875.
    vi.   SUSAN S. BURGESS, b. 1876.

36. MARY ANN ELIZABETH[8] BURGESS *(AGNES ANESS[7] CANNON, ARCHIBALD (JR)[6], ARCHIBALD "ARCHER" (SR)[5], JOHN III[4], JOHN[3], JOHN[2], CANNON FAMILY[1] HISTORY)* was born 23 Feb 1835 in born in Dooly Co., Ga., and died 17 May 1909 in lived in Brooks Co., Ga. most of their lives.. She married OSBORNE BAKER 10 Nov 1850 in Sumter Co., Ga. Lived/ Brooks Co., Ga. most of their lives.. He was born 10 Mar 1930 in Born in Laurens Co., Ga./ Brooks County, and died 02 Feb 1907 in Coolidge, Thomas Co., Georgia..

More About OSBORNE BAKER and MARY BURGESS:
Marriage: 10 Nov 1850, Sumter Co., Ga. Lived/ Brooks Co., Ga. most of their lives.

Children of MARY BURGESS and OSBORNE BAKER are:

      i.   ELIZA ANN[9] BAKER, b. Sep 1851; m. WILLIAM DANIELL.

50.   ii.   JORDAN WESLEY " J. W." BAKER, b. 01 Apr 1853, born in Brooks Co., Ga. READ HIS NOTES; d. 15 May 1934.

      iii. JOHN BUCANNON BAKER, b. 27 Oct 1855.

      iv. JAMES J. BAKER, b. 24 Aug 1858.

      v.   MARY MELVINA BAKER, b. 24 Mar 1861; m. CHARLES DANIELL.

      vi. STEVEN E. "BOSE" BAKER, b. 17 Apr 1865; m. (1) LAURA JANE DUKES, lst Marriage; b. 1869; m. (2) MINNIE DUKES; b. 1875.

          More About STEVEN BAKER and LAURA DUKES:
          Marriage: lst Marriage

      vii. DARLING BAKER, b. 29 Dec 1867.

      viii. DOC MANNING BAKER, b. 08 Nov 1871; m. MARY SHIVER.

      ix. JOSEPH EDDILEE BAKER, b. 27 May 1876.

37. JAMES MADISON[8] BURGESS *(AGNES ANESS[7] CANNON, ARCHIBALD (JR)[6], ARCHIBALD "ARCHER" (SR)[5], JOHN III[4], JOHN[3], JOHN[2], CANNON FAMILY[1] HISTORY)* was born 16 Nov 1843 in Born in Dooly Co., Ga. - Confederate States Army., and died 14 Sep 1923 in of Colquitt Co., PleasantHill Baptist Church Cem. Berlin Ga.. He married ELIZA ANN CAMILE HERNDON 12 Aug 1860 in Dooly Co., Ga. Within l yr after marriage went into CSA War, daughter of GEORGE HERNDON and EDA SHEFFIELD. She was born 1850, and died 1936 in Pleasanthill Baptist Church Cem. Berlin Ga..

Notes for JAMES MADISON BURGESS:
JAMES MADISON BURGESS - 1843-1923

James enlisted in the Wiregrass Rifles or the Brooks County Rifles. He was attached to Company C, 61st Regiment of the Georgia Volunteer Infantry, Gordon's Division, and was a wagoner. CSA- Co C GVI Gordon's Division {Wiregrass Rifles or Brooks Rifles) Captured 6/3/1864. Meckenlenburg, North Carolina. Imprisonment at Petersburg, Virginia. Finally Took Oath of Allienge in 1865 after Civil War Ended to gain Release from Prison. CROSS OF HONOR, IRON CROSS.

During the war he wrote his brother, who lived in Pavo, Georgia, and described battles and warfare. He also mentioned seeing his brother-in-law, OSBORN, who enlisted in the same Regiment. Those letters still exist and are in the care of a Burgess descendant in Pavo, Georgia.

G. W. Nichols' article, "A soldiers Story of His Regiment" states "The 61st carried the Southern Battle Flag farther north than it had ever been carried before in pursuit of the Federals, getting it as far as Wrightsville, Pennsylvania." They captured 5000 Union soldiers. The militia burned the bridge before the Confederates. The 61st then went on to Gettysburg.

On June 3, 1864, James was captured as he rode to Mecklenburg, North Carolina to get commissaries. He was put into prison in Petersburg, Virginia.

James took the Oath of Allegiance in 1865. He said that he had to take the oath to be released from prison. James received the Cross of Honor, Iron Cross for his service in the war.

After the war, James became a farmer and blacksmith in Colquitt County, Georgia. He died in September of 1923, and is buried beside his wife at Pleasant Hill Baptist CHurch Cemetery, Berlin, Ga.

1870 Colquitt Co. Georgia Census

Burgess	James		25 M W	Farm Laborer			Georgia				X	B622
11	101	101	Burgess	Elisa		21 F W	Keeping house			Georgia		
		B622										

12	101	101	Burgess	Elisabeth	3 F W			Georgia				
B622												
13	101	101	Burgess	Rilla	1 F W			Georgia				

More About JAMES BURGESS and ELIZA HERNDON:
Marriage: 12 Aug 1860, Dooly Co., Ga. Within l yr after marriage went into CSA War

Children of JAMES BURGESS and ELIZA HERNDON are:

    i.   JAMES ROBERT[9] BURGESS, b. 1879, Brooks Co. Georgia; m. (1) BELLE TYLER; m. (2) DILLIE CANNON; m. (3) AUTREY BARTLETT, Abt. 1902, Berlin, Colquitt Co. Georgia.

        More About JAMES BURGESS and AUTREY BARTLETT:
        Marriage: Abt. 1902, Berlin, Colquitt Co. Georgia

    ii.   MARY ELIZABETH BURGESS, b. 06 Jun 1866, Berlin Colquitt Co. Georgia; d. 1928; m. (1) WILLIAM T. BURGESS, lst husb.; m. (2) JOHN TYLER.

        More About WILLIAM BURGESS and MARY BURGESS:
        Marriage: lst husb.

51.   iii.   RILLA ETTA BURGESS, b. 25 Oct 1868, born Brooks Co., Ga.; d. 25 Dec 1949, Buried Pleasant Hill Cemetery, Berlin Georgia..

    iv.   SALLIE E. BURGESS, b. 14 Jan 1871, Dade Co. Florida; d. 1962; m. LEONARD HUGHES, Abt. 1892, Dade Co. Florida; d. Lived in Dade Co., Fla..

        More About LEONARD HUGHES and SALLIE BURGESS:
        Marriage: Abt. 1892, Dade Co. Florida

52.   v.   WILLIE ELLA BURGESS, b. 1873; d. 1949, Buried at Pleasant Hill Cemetery, Berlin, Ga..

    vi.   VIRGINIA "JENNIE" BURGESS, b. Bet. 1874 - 1885, Berlin, Colquitt Co. Ga.; m. GEORGE VICKERS.

    vii.   BARRY BURGESS, b. Bet. 1874 - 1885; d. Died at age 5.

    viii.   NETTIE LOVE BURGESS, b. 1886; d. 1957; m. WILLIAM JEFFERSON PLYMALE; b. Plymel(?).

    ix.   LACY LEE BURGESS, b. 1890; d. 1969, Buried at Hopewell Baptist Church Moultrie Ga.; m. SALLIE PILES; b. Pyles(?); d. Buried Hopewell Baptist Church Moultrie Ga..

    x.   JANE BURGESS, b. 1876.

38. REV. GEORGE WASHINGTON[8] CANNON (*JOHN CALHOUN*[7], *ARCHIBALD (JR)*[6], *ARCHIBALD "ARCHER" (SR)*[5], *JOHN III*[4], *JOHN*[3], *JOHN*[2], *CANNON FAMILY*[1] *HISTORY)* was born Jul 1857 in Cen.1860,Sumter Co. Americus, Ga. READ NOTES ON HIM, and died 06 Nov 1936 in Cherokee Co.GA/Murphee Comm/Hwy 319-bet-Thomasville/Moultire GA.. New Hope Freewill Babt.Ch.. He married MARTHA ANN M. (SUSAN) GLASS 01 Apr 1875 in Married in Brooks Co, Ga. Book B, page 145, daughter of JAMES GLASS and JANE SAPP. She was born Jan 1863 in b. Montogomery Co., Ga. SEE George W. Cannon NOTES ON HER., and died 19 Oct 1935 in died Thomas Co., Ga. Death Cert. & Census/ Pleasant Hill Cem..

Notes for REV. GEORGE WASHINGTON CANNON:
George Washington Cannon
 Born in Sumpter County, Georgia; THIS IS HIS ANCESTRY..
son of John Calhoun Cannon of Sumpter Co. Georgia.
    John Calhoun Cannon was born 1816 in Bolloch Co. Georgia.
        Archibald Cannon Jr. born in North Carolina
        Lived in Bulloch Co. Georiga [not in 1860 Bulloch Co Census]
            Archibald Cannon born Pitt Co. N. Carolina; moving to   Georgia to Irwin Co.;
then finally settling in Bulloch Co.   Georgia with his family he died 1820.
            John Cannon, of Surry Co. Virginia. Died in   Wake County North
Carolina. Dec. 1783.
                John Cannon born and died in   Henrico Co. Virginia
                John CANNON First to   come to USA lived in
                Henrico Co. Virginia and   died there.

GEORGE WASHINGTON CANNON - Co. C & E. 10th Battalion "Cranberry Guards", Americus, Ga. Enlisted July 17, 1862. He was a Non-Commissioned Officer - 3rd Sargeant during the Civil War.

He died November 6, 1936 in Burke Co. Ga. He is buried at Murphee's Community off US 319 between Thomasville, Ga. and Moultrie, Ga. New Hope Freewill Baptist Church Cemetery   Ssusan Cannon's death certificate showed her as a WIDOW when she was buried at Pleasanthill Bapt Church. This means he would have had to have died before 1935 although death records were found showing November 6, 1935 in Burke Co. Georgia. [My thought on this is did he move away from Susan and live with another child or relative in his later years?]   George Washington Cannon founded the Prosperity Primitive Baptive Church in Murphee's Church and was the preacher. His grave is found at Murphee's and was made originally as red sandstone which had deplidated over the years.There was a red sticker on the gravesite. The stone has been cracked through the years. This is 5-6 miles before entering Moultrie. In the 1857 Census, Sumter County, Americus, Ga. he would have been three years old. He was listed in that Census with John C. Cannon and Margaret Cannon, parents. Didn't find him in the 1870 Census. He married Martha Ann Glass on April 1, 1875, found in Probate Court, Brooks County, Pavo, Ga., Book B, Page 145. Some of the family members say she was called Susy, although marriage records show Martha Ann M. Glass. Found them together in 1880 Brooks County, in Tallokas District., page 55 of Census, again in 1900 Census, it was later burned in courthouse fire. There are some scattered bits and pieces. Found him again in 1900 Census, Tallokas District, Brooks County, Ga, page 2323. In that Census it gives a birthday, July 1857.

Found in 1910, MIlitia District, 145, Autreyville, Colquitt, Ga., page 601. They had several children.

1920 Federal Census
Surname:Cannon
Given: George W
Birth: Georgia
County: Sumter
Town: Americus
Race: White
Roll: 278
Enum. District: 101
Page: 8B

Relative Lavone & Laurette Cooper of Pavo, Ga. located a lady who knew George Washington Cannon and could still remember where he was buried and she marked it and it is the same grave that both of them saw at New Hope Freewill Baptist Church @ Murphees Community. Lavone and Laurette also have given this researcher a photo of both George Washington Cannon and Martha Ann (Susan) his wife.

Martha Ann M. Glass and George Washington Cannon

UPDATE TO INFORMATION ON GLASS FAMILY September 24, 1996; while searching the history books in the Atlanta History Center Genealogical Library; I found a picture of the GLASS children and the family tree information on the Glass's.

The SUSY, referred to above; IS THE name of the wife according to the records. It is also believed that Susie was half Indian(????) needs to be researched for accuracy.

I am sending you the accurate and factual information as found in the history books. This was submitted to them by EFFIE CLARK GLASS of the Glass family.

Goerge Washington Cannon and his wife and family lived in the area of Berlin - Murphees Community area outside Moultrie. The Cannon family attended the Pleasanthill Baptist Church in Berlin Georgia and several are found buried there. Georgie is not buried with his wife. She choose to be buried at Pleasanthill Baptist Church Cemetery beside hermother and brother's graves. Family tradition is that she wanted to be closer to where her children lived so they could visit her grave.

Several of the CANNON descendants are still in Colquitt County, Georgia and Brooks County, Georgia, Thomas County, Georgia, Hamilton County, Florida and surroudning areas that are descendants of George Washington Cannon and Martha Ann M. Glass known as {Susie or Susan}.

More About REV. GEORGE WASHINGTON CANNON:
Burial: 06 Nov 1936, Burial discrepancy/ Berlin Colquitt Co. Georgia????

Notes for MARTHA ANN M. (SUSAN) GLASS:
GLASS, Martha Ann M. [called Susie or Susan].

Her death certificate gives her age as 78 in 1935. which would have made her date of birth about 1857. This leads to the possibility that she may have been identified as either Mary or Mahala in the 1860 census since the name on her marriage certificate is given as Martha Ann M. Glass.

Tradition is that her full name was Mary Martha Ann which helps to support the theory give above concerning the names and ages shown on the census. She was called Susie or Susan and this is verified by the fact that Susan is given as her name on the death certificate as well as in the 1880, 1900 and 1910 census in which she appears as the wife of George W. Cannon. They had 6 children.

She died October 19, 1935, age 78, while living in Pavo, Georgia with her son Ellis Cannon. [this statement further validates the fact that she was a Widow as stated on death certificate]. The question as to why she did not get buried beside her husband at Murphee's Cemetery on Thomasville Road is by family tradition because she wanted to be buried near her mother who was buried at Pleasanthill Cemetery.

Family tradition is that she is buried in an unmarked grave beside her son CArey F. Cannon at Pleasant Hill Cemetery, Colquitt Georgia. Further verification of the statement of burial place is the fact that Thad CAnnon attended her funeral and told Thelma Bryant Brown a relative that she was buried at Pleasanthill Baptist Church beside her husband.

More About MARTHA ANN M. (SUSAN) GLASS:
Burial: 19 Oct 1935, Buried in unmarked grave beside her son Carey F. Cannon /Plesanthill Cem Colquitt Co. Ga.
Div: 1924, Brooks Co. Ga.

More About REV. CANNON and MARTHA GLASS:
Marriage: 01 Apr 1875, Married in Brooks Co, Ga. Book B, page 145

Children of REV. CANNON and MARTHA GLASS are:
53.   i.   OLLIE MAE[9] CANNON, b. Jan 1880, Brooks Co.GA/Dry Lake 1800 Cen./1900 Cen in home w/parents; d. Both husb & wife Pleasanthill Bapt Cem/Berlin Ga.
          ii. JAMES "JIM" ALLISON CANNON, b. 1874, Born in Colquitt Co., Ga.; d. 09 Jan 1907, Brooks Co. Georgia; m. MAY BELLE SIMMONS, 27 Oct 1907, Brooks Co. Georgia.

               More About JAMES CANNON and MAY SIMMONS:
               Marriage: 27 Oct 1907, Brooks Co. Georgia

          iii. CORRRIE CANNON, b. 1907, Ga.; d. 1951, Sumpter Co. Georgia.
          iv. BILL G. CANNON.
          v.   CHARLES C. CANNON.
          vi. HELEN CANNON.
54.   vii. GEORGIA JOSEPHINE CANNON, b. 28 Apr 1879, Per 1900 cen. records./1910 Cen. Colquitt-Autreyville; d. 23 Apr 1953, Died Colquitt Co/Ga. Pleasant Hill Cem.,Colquitt, GA..
55.   viii. THAD [THADDIE OR THADDIE] N. OR W. CANNON, b. 10 May 1892, born Colquitt Co., Ga. Died in Thomas Co., Ga.; d. 25 Aug 1964, Buried Pleasanthill Bapt Cemetery,Colquitt Co., Ga..
56.   ix. CAREY FRANKLIN SR. CANNON, b. 12 Jul 1894, Berlin Colquitt Co. Ga.; d. 29 Dec 1970, (SSDI) infor. Buried PleasantHill Bapt. Berlin.
57.   x.   ELLIS H. CANNON, b. 26 Mar 1902, Birth date Discrepancy-1900/ Thomasville,Thomas Co. Ga.; d. 12 Sep 1973, Thomas Co., Ga./Sunset Mem. GArdens,Thomasville Ga..

39. CHARLIE [CHARLES] DAVID[8] CANNON *(JOHN CALHOUN[7], ARCHIBALD (JR)[6], ARCHIBALD "ARCHER" (SR)[5], JOHN III[4], JOHN[3], JOHN[2], CANNON FAMILY[1] HISTORY)* was born 1850 in 7 months old in 1850 cen. and 9 yrs old in 1860 cen. He married AMANDA JANE LAMP 04 Jan 1872 in Thomas Georgia, daughter of LEWIS LAMP and JANE CANNON. She was born 1852.

More About CHARLIE CANNON and AMANDA LAMP:
Marriage: 04 Jan 1872, Thomas Georgia

Children of CHARLIE CANNON and AMANDA LAMP are:
          i.   SUSAN "SUSIE" E.[9] CANNON, b. 23 Jan 1876; m. JOHN JORDAN.
          ii. LAURA CANNON, b. 1878.
          iii. ROSA BELL CANNON, b. 14 Dec 1891; d. 13 Apr 1926, Salem Cem/Pavo,Brooks Co. Ga.; m. TARK ELISHA GLOVER; b. 09 Mar 1881, Son of ELijah Glover and Frances Vonier; d. 22 Feb 1972, Salem Cem/Pavo,Brooks Co. Ga..

     iv.   AMANDA CANNON, m. JOHN GLOVER.
     v.   VERSIE CANNON.
     vi.   HENRY MORGAN CANNON, b. 14 May 1885.

40. DANIEL JAMES[8] CANNON *(JAMES M. [JIMPSEY][7], ARCHIBALD (JR)[6], ARCHIBALD "ARCHER" (SR)[5], JOHN III[4], JOHN[3], JOHN[2], CANNON FAMILY[1] HISTORY)* was born 21 Oct 1848 in Georgia, and died 22 Dec 1920 in Colquitt Co. Ga.. He married LOUISIANA HANNEY. She was born 30 Dec 1858 in Georgia, and died 01 Oct 1906 in Colquitt Co. Ga..

Children of DANIEL CANNON and LOUISIANA HANNEY are:
     i.   ESSIE[9] CANNON, m. OTIS COOPER.
     ii.   VANDELLA CANNON.
     iii.   ATTIE CANNON.
     iv.   ELLA CANNON.
     v.   VETTIE CANNON.
     vi.   ODIE CANNON.

41. RANDALL ROAN[8] CANNON *(JAMES M. [JIMPSEY][7], ARCHIBALD (JR)[6], ARCHIBALD "ARCHER" (SR)[5], JOHN III[4], JOHN[3], JOHN[2], CANNON FAMILY[1] HISTORY)* was born 05 Jan 1850 in Sumpter Co. Ga., and died 08 May 1929 in Altha Calhoun Co. Ga./Pleasanthill BApt Colquitt Co GA Cem.. He married SARAH ANN HARDWICK in Sumpter Co. Georgia. She was born 25 Mar 1856 in Sumpter Co. Georgia, and died 10 Nov 1922 in Colquitt Co. GA/Pleasanthill BApt Cem..

More About RANDALL CANNON and SARAH HARDWICK:
Marriage: Sumpter Co. Georgia

Children of RANDALL CANNON and SARAH HARDWICK are:
     i.   LULA MOZELLE[9] CANNON, b. 12 Sep 1875.
     ii.   DANIEL CANNON, b. 09 Jan 1877.
     iii.   RENTZ CANNON, b. 17 Nov 1888.
     iv.   ARTHUR CANNON, b. 02 Feb 1880.
     v.   JAMES CANNON, b. 28 Apr 1882.
     vi.   EDWARD CANNON, b. 11 Jul 1884.
     vii.   MILLIE CANNON, b. 03 Nov 1886.
     viii.   HAMMOND J. CANNON, b. 20 Nov 1888.
     ix.   EMILY E. CANNON, b. Abt. 1892.
     x.   LESSIE L. CANNON, b. 06 Jan 1899.
     xi.   ETTA CANNON, b. May 1894.

42. ROXANNA ROSETTA[8] CANNON *(JAMES M. [JIMPSEY][7], ARCHIBALD (JR)[6], ARCHIBALD "ARCHER" (SR)[5], JOHN III[4], JOHN[3], JOHN[2], CANNON FAMILY[1] HISTORY)* was born 1856. She married JOSEPH E. H. JORDAN 04 Jan 1877 in Brooks Co. Georgia. He was born 1857 in Brooks Co. Georgia.

More About JOSEPH JORDAN and ROXANNA CANNON:
Marriage: 04 Jan 1877, Brooks Co. Georgia

Children of ROXANNA CANNON and JOSEPH JORDAN are:
     i.   EMILY[9] JORDAN, b. 1877.
     ii.   SOLOMON JORDAN, b. 1879.

43. SARAH SERNA[8] CANNON *(JAMES M. [JIMPSEY][7], ARCHIBALD (JR)[6], ARCHIBALD "ARCHER" (SR)[5], JOHN III[4], JOHN[3], JOHN[2], CANNON FAMILY[1] HISTORY)* was born 30 Apr 1857 in Georgia, and died 15 Apr 1936 in Prosperity Cem/Ione,Brooks Co. Ga.. She married JAMES F. HERNDON in Brooks Co. Georgia. He was born 09 Oct 1853, and died 05 Sep 1937 in Prosperity Cem/Ione Brooks Co. Ga..

More About JAMES HERNDON and SARAH CANNON:
Marriage: Brooks Co. Georgia

Child of SARAH CANNON and JAMES HERNDON is:
      i.   JARVIE[9] HERNDON, b. 24 Mar 1881, Brooks Co. Georgia; d. 11 Nov 1897, Prosperity Cem/Brooks Co.
           Georgia.

44. AMANDA JANE[8] LAMP *(JANE[7] CANNON, ARCHIBALD (JR)[6], ARCHIBALD "ARCHER" (SR)[5], JOHN III[4], JOHN[3], JOHN[2], CANNON FAMILY[1] HISTORY)* was born 1852. She married CHARLIE [CHARLES] DAVID CANNON 04 Jan 1872 in Thomas Georgia, son of JOHN CANNON and MARGARET JETT. He was born 1850 in 7 months old in 1850 cen. and 9 yrs old in 1860 cen.

More About CHARLIE CANNON and AMANDA LAMP:
Marriage: 04 Jan 1872, Thomas Georgia

Children are listed above under (39) Charlie [Charles] David Cannon.

45. SERENA[8] CANNON *(JOHNATHAN R.[7], DEMPSEY[6], ARCHIBALD "ARCHER" (SR)[5], JOHN III[4], JOHN[3], JOHN[2], CANNON FAMILY[1] HISTORY)* was born 29 Sep 1848 in Bulloch Georgia, and died 30 Aug 1881 in Corinth Cemetery, Ft. Stewart, Ga. Bryan Co. Georgia. She married ELIJAH E. SHUMAN 26 Nov 1865 in Bryan Co. Georgia. He was born 07 Jun 1842 in Bryan Co. Ga., and died 05 May 1893 in Bryan Co. Georgia.

More About ELIJAH SHUMAN and SERENA CANNON:
Marriage: 26 Nov 1865, Bryan Co. Georgia

Child of SERENA CANNON and ELIJAH SHUMAN is:
      i.   RAYMOND DEMERY[9] SHUMAN, b. 29 Aug 1868, Bryan Co. Georgia; d. 18 Mar 1940, Bryan Co.
           Georgia.

46. JAMES WILIAM[8] CANNON *(JOHNATHAN R.[7], DEMPSEY[6], ARCHIBALD "ARCHER" (SR)[5], JOHN III[4], JOHN[3], JOHN[2], CANNON FAMILY[1] HISTORY)* was born 1851 in Bryan Co. Georgia, and died 16 May 1909 in 1880 Cen/Bryan Co. Ga.. He married SARAH MISSISIPPI SMITH in Bryan Co. Ga.. She was born 1855, and died 16 Nov 1908.

More About JAMES CANNON and SARAH SMITH:
Marriage: Bryan Co. Ga.

Children of JAMES CANNON and SARAH SMITH are:
      i.   SHEPARD[9] CANNON, b. 1873.
      ii. SARAH CANNON, b. 1875.
     iii. HENRY J. CANNON, b. 1878.
     iv. GENERAL CANNON, b. 1879.

47. JOHN ROBERT[8] CANNON *(WILLIAM A.[7], DEMPSEY[6], ARCHIBALD "ARCHER" (SR)[5], JOHN III[4], JOHN[3], JOHN[2], CANNON FAMILY[1] HISTORY)* was born Abt. 1848 in Bulloch Co. Ga., and died 04 Nov 1910 in Bulloch Co. Ga.. He married ANN JANE MCELVEEN. She was born Abt. 1849, and died 27 Oct 1919.

Children of JOHN CANNON and ANN MCELVEEN are:
      i.   ONIE BELL[9] CANNON, b. 17 Mar 1881, Bulloch Co. Ga.; m. JESSIE LEE FLOYD, 01 Aug 1901,
           Bulloch Co. Ga..

           More About JESSIE FLOYD and ONIE CANNON:
           Marriage: 01 Aug 1901, Bulloch Co. Ga.

    ii.   PURIFOY CANNON, b. 13 Mar 1884.

48. NATHAN A.[8] CANNON *(WILLIAM A.[7], DEMPSEY[6], ARCHIBALD "ARCHER" (SR)[5], JOHN III[4], JOHN[3], JOHN[2], CANNON FAMILY[1] HISTORY)* was born 27 Dec 1853 in Bryan Co. Ga., and died 02 May 1916 in Bryan Co. Georgia. He married CLARA E. SHUMAN 18 Dec 1878 in Bryan Co. Ga. Marriage, daughter of JOHN SHUMAN and ELIZABETH HARVEY.

More About NATHAN CANNON and CLARA SHUMAN:
Marriage: 18 Dec 1878, Bryan Co. Ga. Marriage

Children of NATHAN CANNON and CLARA SHUMAN are:
    i.   CLYDE[9] CANNON, b. Abt. 1892, Bryan Co. Ga..
    ii.   ROBERT CANNON, b. Abt. 1894, Bryan Co. Ga..

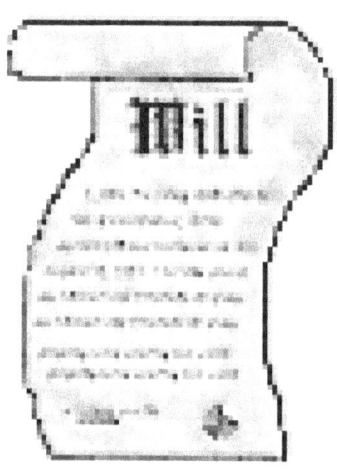

Generation No. 9

49. WILLIAM HENRY[9] CANNON *(JOHN S.[8], HENRY B.[7], JOHN[6], ARCHIBALD "ARCHER" (SR)[5], JOHN III[4], JOHN[3], JOHN[2], CANNON FAMILY[1] HISTORY)* was born 12 Dec 1851 in Texas, and died 27 Oct 1929 in Ellis Co Texas. He married SARAH 'KATHERINE' KATE FORTUNE 16 Jul 1881 in Ellis Co. Texas.

More About WILLIAM CANNON and SARAH FORTUNE:
Marriage: 16 Jul 1881, Ellis Co. Texas

Children of WILLIAM CANNON and SARAH FORTUNE are:
- i. EUNICE[10] CANNON, b. Abt. 1883, TX; d. Abt. 1954, Dallas Co. TX.
- ii. RICHARD EDGAR CANNON, b. 18 Nov 1884, Italy Ellis Co Texas.
- iii. WILLIAM HENRY CANNON, b. 01 Dec 1886, Texas; d. 17 Mar 1962, Los Angeles California.
- iv. BENJAMIN ELLIS CANNON, b. 31 Jul 1888, Texas; d. Aug 1977, Dawson Navarro Texas.
- v. JOHN ROBERT CANNON, b. 13 Jan 1891, Italy Ellis Co Texas; d. 28 Dec 1860, Temple Beall Co. Texas.
- vi. MAJORIE KATHERINE "MARGIE" CANNON, b. 12 Jan 1906, Italy Ellis Co. Texas; d. 08 Feb 1975, Corsicana Nvarro Texas.

50. JORDAN WESLEY " J. W."[9] BAKER *(MARY ANN ELIZABETH[8] BURGESS, AGNES ANESS[7] CANNON, ARCHIBALD (JR)[6], ARCHIBALD "ARCHER" (SR)[5], JOHN III[4], JOHN[3], JOHN[2], CANNON FAMILY[1] HISTORY)* was born 01 Apr 1853 in born in Brooks Co., Ga. READ HIS NOTES, and died 15 May 1934. He married AMANDA CAROLINE DUKES 15 Apr 1877 in Brooks Co., Ga., daughter of MOSES DUKE and SARAH EDWARDS. She was born 1861, and died 11 Dec 1946 in Brooks Co., Ga..

Notes for JORDAN WESLEY " J. W." BAKER:
Baker, Jordan Wesley--- was born April 1, 1853 in Laurens Co., Ga. his father Osborne Baker and his mother was Mary Ann Burgess, the daughter of Dillard Burgess. In the 1850's the family came to the Tallokas area of Brooks County from Sumter County, Ga.

   J. W. married Amanda C. Dukes, the daughter of Moses Dukes of Brooks County, Ga. The farming family had eight children.

   Jordan and Amanda had one daughter in 1880 who died as an infant. Jordan and Amanda lived in Brooks County until their deaths. Both are buried at Harmony Church near Barwick, Ga. There parents are buried there also.

More About JORDAN BAKER and AMANDA DUKES:
Marriage: 15 Apr 1877, Brooks Co., Ga.

Children of JORDAN BAKER and AMANDA DUKES are:
- i. MATTIE[10] BAKER, b. 31 Jan 1879; m. (1) LEE ROGERS, lst husb.; m. (2) SHERMAN GUNTER, 2nd Husb./Colquitt Co., Ga. Marriage.

  More About LEE ROGERS and MATTIE BAKER:
  Marriage: lst husb.

  More About SHERMAN GUNTER and MATTIE BAKER:
  Marriage: 2nd Husb./Colquitt Co., Ga. Marriage

- ii. HENNIE MOZELL BAKER, b. 10 May 1882; m. (1) JAKE I. HOLLOWAY, lst Husb.; m. (2) JOHN LOCKE ELMORE, 2nd Husb..

  More About JAKE HOLLOWAY and HENNIE BAKER:
  Marriage: lst Husb.

  More About JOHN ELMORE and HENNIE BAKER:
  Marriage: 2nd Husb.

	iii.	JAMES WESLEY BAKER, b. 13 Feb 1884; m. EDNA STRICKLAND.
58.	iv.	JOHN OSBORNE BAKER, b. 10 Oct 1885, born in Thomas Co., Ga.; d. 30 May 1948, Brooks Co., Ga..
	v.	CHARLIE E. BAKER, b. 16 Nov 1887; m. EULA ROGERS.
	vi.	WILLIAM LACEY BAKER, b. 27 Feb 1890; m. ALMA HOLLOWAY, Jan 1911.

More About WILLIAM BAKER and ALMA HOLLOWAY:
Marriage: Jan 1911

	vii.	FRANK DELENO BAKER, b. 12 Feb 1892; m. LIZZIE WHEELER, Sep 1916, Brooks Co., Ga..

More About FRANK BAKER and LIZZIE WHEELER:
Marriage: Sep 1916, Brooks Co., Ga.

59.	viii.	MANOR IVERSON BAKER, b. 13 Mar 1894, Brooks Co., Ga.; d. 26 Sep 1971.

51. RILLA ETTA[9] BURGESS *(JAMES MADISON[8], AGNES ANESS[7] CANNON, ARCHIBALD (JR)[6], ARCHIBALD "ARCHER" (SR)[5], JOHN III[4], JOHN[3], JOHN[2], CANNON FAMILY[1] HISTORY)* was born 25 Oct 1868 in born Brooks Co., Ga., and died 25 Dec 1949 in Buried Pleasant Hill Cemetery, Berlin Georgia.. She married JAMES GORDON GLASS 15 Oct 1831 in Quitman, Brooks Co, Ga. Book B page 515, son of JAMES GLASS and JANE SAPP. He was born 25 Feb 1857 in Born Mitchell Co, Ga./1 yr old in 1860 census. SEE MORE, and died 14 Sep 1932 in Pleasanthill Baptist Church Cemetery A Farmer..

Notes for JAMES GORDON GLASS:
JAMES Gordon GLASS - 1859 - 1923 MITCHELL Co, Ga.

JAMES GLASS - 1859 - 1923 MITCHELL Co, Ga.

James Gordon Glass was born Feb. 25, 1859 in Mitchell Co., Ga. He was the son of James Glass and his wife, Jane Sapp. He grew up to manhood in the vicinity of the area where he was born. He was a farmer. In the 1860 Census, he and his family lived in Mitchell County, Ga. He married and had five children.

Jane's last name was Sapp. A Charity Sapp verified her pension application for James Glass after his death. See his notes.

Effie Clark Glass of Brandon, Florida submitted this data.

James Gordon Glass was born Feb. 25, 1859 in Mitchell Co., Ga. He was the son of James Glass and his wife, Jane Sapp. He grew up to manhood in the vicinity of the area where he was born. He was a farmer.

He married and had eleven children all born in Georgia..

Jane's last name has now been found. It is SAPP. A Charity Sapp verified her pension application for James Glass after his death. See his notes.

Effie Clark Glass of Brandon, Florida submitted this data.

FOUND A PICTURE OF JAMES GORDON GLASS AND RILLA BURGESS GLASS. WHAT A FIND!!!!!

More About JAMES GORDON GLASS:
Census: 1900, in cen living with Jane his mother Colquitt Co. Ga.

More About JAMES GLASS and RILLA BURGESS:
Marriage: 15 Oct 1831, Quitman, Brooks Co, Ga. Book B page 515

Children of RILLA BURGESS and JAMES GLASS are:

      i.   ADA LOVE[10] GLASS, b. 05 Aug 1883, born Mitchell Co. GA; d. 24 Jan 1951, Wesley Chapel Methodist CHurch Cem, Berlin, Ga.; m. EDGAR EUGENE TYLER, 17 Feb 1951, Colquitt Co. GA; d. 01 Jan 1941, Wesley Chapel Methodist CHurch Cem, Berlin, Ga..

           More About EDGAR TYLER and ADA GLASS:
           Marriage: 17 Feb 1951, Colquitt Co. GA

      ii. ETTA DOVE GLASS, b. Bet. 1883 - 1902, Died in childhood.; d. Died YOUNG..
     iii. TALLY GLASS, b. Bet. 1883 - 1902, Died in Childhood.; d. Died Young..

60.   iv. JAMES "BOB" ROBERT GLASS, b. 24 Feb 1886, Born in Georgia. SEE NOTES.; d. 17 Aug 1963, Hopewell Baptist Church Cem. Moultrie, Ga..

      v. JOSEPH FRANKLIN GLASS, b. 18 Feb 1889, Born S. Carolina; d. 28 Sep 1976, He died in Seneca, Oconee Co., South Carolina.; m. RUTH IONE (PEARL) WHITWORTH, Lived in Westminister, S.C.; b. who lived in Westminister. South Carolina.; d. Buried in South Carolina..

           More About JOSEPH GLASS and RUTH WHITWORTH:
           Marriage: Lived in Westminister, S.C.

      vi. HARMON GORDON GLASS, b. 25 Jun 1892, World War I Veteran-Brooks County Rolls; d. 07 Aug 1969, Pleasanthill Baptist Church Cemetery, Berlin, Ga.; m. MAE TOUCHTON, 20 Feb 1920; b. 05 Mar 1890, Echols Co, Ga.; d. 13 Oct 1969, Pleasanthill Baptist Church Cemetery, Berlin, Ga..

           More About HARMON GLASS and MAE TOUCHTON:
           Marriage: 20 Feb 1920

61.   vii. NOAH ELDON GLASS, b. 09 Aug 1894; d. 19 May 1951, Pleasanthill Baptist CHurch Cemetery, Berlin, Ga..

     viii. JULIE BELLE GLASS, b. 30 Oct 1896, Ga.; d. 30 Oct 1984, Buried with Levin;Statenville - Echols, Ga.; m. (1) P. CLEVER WILKES; m. (2) LEVIN (LEWIS) G. TOUCHTON; d. Buried with Julie; Echols, Ga..

      ix. WILLIAM CASON GLASS, b. 04 Apr 1898; d. 20 Jan 1978, 1918(?); m. LYDIA WEBB, 20 Jan 1918.

           More About WILLIAM GLASS and LYDIA WEBB:
           Marriage: 20 Jan 1918

62.   x. LULA LEE GLASS, b. 04 Nov 1901; d. 1984, Okapilco Baptist Church Cem, Quitman, Ga..

      xi. BEULAH MAE GLASS, b. 25 Dec 1902; d. 22 Dec 1970, Pleasanthill Baptist Church, Berlin, Ga.; m. (1) CECIL BOZEMAN; m. (2) LEE BISHOP; d. Pleasanthill Baptist Church, Berlin, Ga..

52. WILLIE ELLA[9] BURGESS *(JAMES MADISON[8], AGNES ANESS[7] CANNON, ARCHIBALD (JR)[6], ARCHIBALD "ARCHER" (SR)[5], JOHN III[4], JOHN[3], JOHN[2], CANNON FAMILY[1] HISTORY)* was born 1873, and died 1949 in Buried at Pleasant Hill Cemetery, Berlin, Ga.. She married JOSEPH C. BOYD.

Child of WILLIE BURGESS and JOSEPH BOYD is:
      i.   BARBARA[10] BOYD, b. 09 Aug 1894; d. 19 May 1951.

53. OLLIE MAE[9] CANNON *(REV. GEORGE WASHINGTON[8], JOHN CALHOUN[7], ARCHIBALD (JR)[6], ARCHIBALD "ARCHER" (SR)[5], JOHN III[4], JOHN[3], JOHN[2], CANNON FAMILY[1] HISTORY)* was born Jan 1880 in Brooks Co.GA/Dry Lake 1800 Cen./1900 Cen in home w/parents, and died in Both husb & wife Pleasanthill Bapt Cem/Berlin Ga. She married WILLIAM W. GOLDMAN 15 Oct 1899 in Brooks County, Ga. Book E, Pg 73. He was born 1872 in Georgia- res:1920-Tallokas Brooks Co.Ga, and died in Has a slab -no name or inscription on it..

Notes for OLLIE MAE CANNON:
Ollie Cannon was the Sister of Carey Franklin Cannon and her ancestral line would be the same as for him. Ollie is both Aunt and great-grandmother to his children by his marriage to Winnnifred Lauretta Goldman.

According to history of Pleasant Hill Baptist Church both W. W. "Bud" Goldman and Ollie Cannon Goldman are buried there and their graves are covered with concrete markers with no inscriptions.

More About WILLIAM GOLDMAN and OLLIE CANNON:
Marriage: 15 Oct 1899, Brooks County, Ga. Book E, Pg 73

Children of OLLIE CANNON and WILLIAM GOLDMAN are:
    i.   HOBSON EUGENE[10] GOLDMAN.
    ii. CLYDE GOLDMAN.
    iii. BLANCHE GOLDMAN.
    iv. IDELLA GOLDMAN.

54. GEORGIA JOSEPHINE[9] CANNON *(REV. GEORGE WASHINGTON[8], JOHN CALHOUN[7], ARCHIBALD (JR)[6], ARCHIBALD "ARCHER" (SR)[5], JOHN III[4], JOHN[3], JOHN[2], CANNON FAMILY[1] HISTORY)* was born 28 Apr 1879 in Per 1900 cen. records./1910 Cen. Colquitt-Autreyville, and died 23 Apr 1953 in Died Colquitt Co/Ga. Pleasant Hill Cem.,Colquitt, GA.. She married JOHN HENRY HITCH BRYANT 23 Jan 1898 in Brooks Co. Book WE p. 46 13 yrs w/lst cd, son of JOHN BRYANT and MARTHA GILES. He was born 27 Sep 1871 in READ NOTES/Familytreemaker Vol. III-Tree#0951, and died 16 Jan 1968 in Jan18,1968Pleasant Hill Cem Colquitt, GA. Died at age 96..

Notes for GEORGIA JOSEPHINE CANNON:
Georgie J. Cannon - was not shown in the 1880 Census, but showed up in 1900 Census. In that census it shows she was born April , 1879, but her headstone shows, April 25, 1886. She married John Henry Hitch Bryant, January 23, 1898 in Brooks County, Book WE, page 46. Even though she was married she was still listed in the 1900 Census with her parents. The 1900 Census listed her as being born 1879, which is seven years difference. (Opinion, believe it is closer to being right - because she would have been only 12 years old at the time she was married), however, this is possible because women did marry at that early of an age back during these time periods. She was age 13 yrs when her first child was born.

My grandmother died April 23, 1953 I, Lanette (Brown) (Kirkland) Hill was born, daughter of Thelma Bryant on May 2, 1953 only a few days after her death.

More About GEORGIA JOSEPHINE CANNON:
Census: 1900, Shown in home of her parents even though she was married.

Notes for JOHN HENRY HITCH BRYANT:
JOHN HENRY HITCH BRYANT -

John H. Bryant, born Georgia; age 49 in 1920 Federal Census of Colquit Co., Ga. White/Colquitt - Moultrie area; District 17. Born year 1871.

He was born on County Line/Colquitt County, Georgia (between Colquitt and Brooks County). The Bryants used to own lots of property in Moultrie. They owned a farm in Colquitt County off Rosencraft Road near Elizabeth Glass's home in Moultrie. Where did the name "Hitch" come from? My guess is that he is named after the Doctor, Robert M. Hitch and family from Morven Community, in Brooks County, Ga. I believe that this doctor delivered him into this world. I will check this out with the oldest family members to learn more information on this.
    Dr. Robert Marcuss Hitch served as a Confederate Officer and settled in Morven in 1864. He was a Surgeon of the Army of Tennessee.

When he was little, he told the family that he witnessed a killing. After the Civil War, there was still a racial indifference in South Georgia. Due to the lack of better law enforcement at that time in history the following story took place and as a young boy he witnessed a horrible killing. There was a black man that had raped and killed a little white girl while she was walking to store in Autreyville to get snuff for her mother. He then strapped body to a log in the little pond (off dirt) about 2 miles to store. She was reported missing and went to hunting her. Her body was found in the pond when her sister while at the pond, stepped on the log in the water and the little girls body floated out from under the log. So the men in the Autreyville, Ga. area had grouped together to find him and when they did, they cut off body parts and made him eat them before finally killing him by fire. The black man admitted to killing the little girl. There was no law back then and these kinds of cruelty went on in the communities. This incident was reported to the law, but no legal proceedings were ever held against the men of the community.

This incident really affected him so badly, he talked about how horrible it was to see being done to his family members and it affected him all his life.

There is was another John Henry Bryant that was Black living at the same time in Colquitt County who was arrested and convicted of murder. The record in the following WAS NOT OUR grandfather. John Henry Bryant (Black) was held in Colquitt County, Georgia & convicted for Co-Conspirator with Baggett, Berry. However,application was filed to the Governor for Clemency. 1858 - 1942. Georgia Black Book. Vol. I. I wanted to make sure that this bad record was not my great-grandfather, so I went and looked at the original documents in the Georgia Archives, Atlanta, Georgia 9-8-2000 and read and saw that this was indeed NOT our family member as the man in question was a Black man who lived in the area at the same time. Telephoned family to let them know the good news!!

Notes by Parrish, grand-son.
Parish stated that he and Violet kept g'pa when he took down [meaning got sick]. Violet shaving him, to town haircut, etc., he was getting read, she went after the car, heard a fall, she ran back and tried to get him up, he said "honey don't brother, I'm dying". Last words he spoke.

He was 98 years old. In bed - 5-6 weeks, couldn't speak, stroke one side other side gangreen in legs. Using Dr. King. (This was the 2nd stroke papa Bryant had). He'd get a little better, he used a little ball to exercise his hands. Started hoeing up grass. "Couldn't keep him still". They'd plant grass and he'd hoe it up. He said, "I can't stand to see grass grow under my feet." Here he comes with the hoe over his shoulder. Dr. said, "let him go". G'pa said after hoeing up grass, "I've got it now where y'all can come and go's walking on grass." Violet stated to him, "Mr. Bryant we set out that grass." We never said anything else about him hoeing up the grass.

G'ma died at Austin's place. Austin stayed drunk. He told g'pa he'd have to get out. Mr. Anderson Preacher, he was preaching at Emerald Hill, came to see Parish, told him g'pa was not being looked after, bad shape. Parish went after him. He had strokes. June and Irene came, talked, offered to keep him some. Two weeks each place. Irene will help out. Susie kept him some, but he and Rob would get drunk, Austin would get him and they'd end up drunk.

June was upset, he looked too young to be "laid out Junes house". "It just ain't Pa" Irene trying to help make arrangements - June mad and Irene would cry.

Grandma (Jack Both - Gregory_ she had some insurance and g'pa did. Parish, Austin, June paid funeral arrangements.

Grand-ma stated to Violet, "When I die, I don't want anyone crying over me." "I'm going to a better place." A little later, stomach swelling up and getting bigger (Dr. Daniels) finally cath. But the swelling continued. Afterwards it wasn't too long when she passed away. Grandpa and Austin all doped up - something Dr. Daniels had given them. "Some thing to hold them up I guess", he stated, both crazy acting. Quoted by Violet. Violet, June and Dot was with her when she died. Litt went after Parrish.

JOHN HENRY BRYANT TAKEN BY DEATH SERVICES FRIDAY

John Henry Bryant, 96 years old of Sunset Community, died Tuesday night at Brooks County Hospital after an illness of five weeks. Funeral services will be held Friday at 3:00 p.m. at Pleasant Hill Baptist Church in Colquitt County. Burial will be in the church cemetery. The Rev. Julian T. Maddox and the Rev. J. R. Sellars will officiate at the services.

Mr. Bryant was a retired farmer and was a member of Northside Baptist Church in Quitman, Ga. Survivors include four sons; J. T. Bryant, Parrish Bryant, Quitman, Ivey Bryant, Thomasville, Austin

Bryant, Valdosta; six daughters: Mrs. Josephine Dees, Mrs. Florence Cook, Mrs. Myrtice Littles, all of Moultrie, Mrs. Susie Jordan, Barwick, Mrs. Ollie Grubbs, Perry, Florida, Mrs. Kathleen Clemons, Greensboro,N.C.

Forty-four grandchildren, 78 great-grandchildren and 10 great-great-grandchildren also survive.

The 1920 Federal Census reflects a John Henry Bryant White, age 49 living in Colquitt/Moultrie area born 1871.

More About JOHN HENRY HITCH BRYANT:
Census: 1920, Joh HH Bryant is listed.

More About JOHN BRYANT and GEORGIA CANNON:
Marriage: 23 Jan 1898, Brooks Co. Book WE p. 46 13 yrs w/lst cd

Children of GEORGIA CANNON and JOHN BRYANT are:

      i.   JOSEPHINE[10] BRYANT, b. As of 9/2000 lives at Sunset Home in Moultrie, Ga.; d. 26 Apr 2004, Berlin/Pleasanthill Bapt Church Cem. Georgia; m. CLARENCE CANNON.

          More About JOSEPHINE BRYANT:
          Burial: Not buried w/Clarence.

63.   ii.   KATHERINE BRYANT, d. 1920.
64.   iii.   PARRISH BRYANT, b. 24 Mar 1869, READ HIS NOTES ABOUT John Henry Hitch Bryant TOO.; d. 14 Feb 1911, Buried at Schley in Colquitt County, Ga..
65.   iv.   WILLIAM FRANKLIN BRYANT, b. 25 May 1899, Colquitt Co., Ga.; d. 15 May 1937, 38 yrs old. Pleasant HIll Cemetery,Colquitt, GA..
66.   v.   OLLIE LIVINIA BRYANT, b. 08 Jun 1901, Colquitt Co. Ga.; d. 1975.
67.   vi.   IVEY JOHN BRYANT, b. 07 May 1903, Colquitt, Ga. - /WWI/Served in the ARMY.; d. 11 Jul 1974, Died 71 yrs Pleasanthill Babt/Church Cem.Berlin, Ga..
    vii.   SUSIE BRYANT, b. 22 Sep 1905, Colquitt County, Ga.; d. 31 Mar, Kennedy Chapel Cemetery in Coolidge; m. ROB JORDAN, 1947.

          More About ROB JORDAN and SUSIE BRYANT:
          Marriage: 1947

68. viii. FLORENCE FLOSSIE BRYANT, b. 31 Oct 1906, Colquitt, Co.,Ga. READ HER NOTES; d. 25 Apr 1995, Cook Plot-Greenfield Cemetery,Moultrie,Ga..
     ix.   CALVIN D. BRYANT, b. 15 Jul 1909, Colquitt Co. Ga; d. 29 Dec 1970, Buried Pleasanthill Cemetery, Colquitt Co., Ga.; m. ALICE; b. 1896; d. 1943, Buried Pleasanthill Bapt Church Cem.

          More About ALICE:
          Burial: an infant buried beside her w/no name on slab.

69.   x.   JUNE TRAVIS BRYANT, b. 01 Jun 1918, Lived in Eastman, Georgia. (Died of sudden heart attack); d. 15 Dec 2000, Died Columbus, Ga. Buried/Moultrie Cem. near Sunrise Nurs Georgia.
70.   xi.   AUSTIN WESLEY BRYANT, b. 18 Sep 1921, Named after Dr. Austin in Pavo, Georgia.; d. 26 Jul 1992, Deceased-Cancer, Pleasant Hill Cematery,Berlin Ga.
71.   xii. LINNIE MYRTICE BRYANT, b. 26 Sep 1924, Born Colquitt County, Ga. Lived in Moultrie, Georgia..

55. THAD [THADDIE OR THADDIE] N. OR W.[9] CANNON *(REV. GEORGE WASHINGTON[8], JOHN CALHOUN[7], ARCHIBALD (JR)[6], ARCHIBALD "ARCHER" (SR)[5], JOHN III[4], JOHN[3], JOHN[2], CANNON FAMILY[1] HISTORY)* was born 10 May 1892 in born Colquitt Co., Ga. Died in Thomas Co., Ga., and died 25 Aug 1964 in Buried Pleasanthill Bapt Cemetery,Colquitt Co., Ga.. He married (1) EMMA MCCORMICK.   He married (2) NEELY MCKINNEY 24 Dec 1912 in Thad lst Husband. Colquitt Co. Georgia. She was born 05 Oct 1897, and died 27 Jan 1991 in Buried Pleasant Hill Bapt Church Cemetery,Colquitt Co., Ga./Berlin.

More About THAD CANNON and NEELY MCKINNEY:

Marriage: 24 Dec 1912, Thad lst Husband. Colquitt Co. Georgia

Children of THAD CANNON and NEELY McKINNEY are:

	i.	ESTELL[10] CANNON, m. GEORGE ADAMS.
	ii.	RALPH CANNON, m. LUCILLE.
72.	iii.	EVELYN CANNON, d. Nov 1999, Pleasanthill Babtis Cem. Berlin Ga..
	iv.	LONNIE CANNON, m. MAE; b. from Orlando.
	v.	BUDDIE (R.V.) CANNON, b. 07 Aug 1926, Born in Colquitt County, Ga. READ HIS NOTES; d. 25 Jul 1984, Colquitt Co., G.a Pleasanthill Baptist Church Cemetery; m. VERTIE; b. Layton Glass's lst wife..

Notes for BUDDIE (R.V.) CANNON:
R. V. Cannon - Aug. 7, 1926 - July 25, 1984

Funeral services were for R. V. (Buddy) Cannon, 57, were conducted today at Bethlehem Free Will Baptist Church. The Rev. Joe Owens officiated. Burial was in Pleasanthill Baptist Church Cemetery.

Mr. Cannon died Monday at the Veterans Administration Hospital in Lake City, Florida, after a lengthy illness. A FARMER, he made his home on Route 5, Moultrie, Georgia.

Pallbearers were: Billy Kent, Chuck English, Ricky Kent, West Carter, Jerry Cannon and Roger Cannon.

A native of Colquitt County, Georgia, he was born August 7, 1926. He was the son of Thad Cannon and Neely McKinney Cannon.

He is survived by his wife, Mrs. Verdie Cannon, Route 5, Moultrie, Ga.; mother, Mrs. Neeley Cannon; Berlin; one step-daughter - Linda Yawn of Gainesville, Fla; two brothers; Ralph Cannon, Moultrie and Evelyn Kent of Berlin, Ga.

A note from email received from Larry Cannon of Dallas, Tx.; states "R. V. (Buddy) Cannon was in Houston chasing after Winifred Goldman Cannon who was married to grandfather Carey and had 3 kids at the time. This was in '55 and '56. Winifred and Aunt Peggy (Pauline Emma Cannon) ran off to New Orleans andleft gf Carey with the kids. Buddy followed them there. I don't know what happened after that because they were still in New Orleans when I joined the Marines in '57.

56. CAREY FRANKLIN SR.[9] CANNON *(REV. GEORGE WASHINGTON[8], JOHN CALHOUN[7], ARCHIBALD (JR)[6], ARCHIBALD "ARCHER" (SR)[5], JOHN III[4], JOHN[3], JOHN[2], CANNON FAMILY[1] HISTORY)* was born 12 Jul 1894 in Berlin Colquitt Co. Ga., and died 29 Dec 1970 in (SSDI) infor. Buried PleasantHill Bapt. Berlin. He married (1) RUTH EVELYN "PAULINE" SIMMONS 29 Jun 1913 in lst wife. Colquitt Co. Georgia. She was born 18 May 1897 in liberty CO. Ludowici Georgia. He married (2) WINNIFRED LAURETTA GOLDMAN 25 Jan 1946 in Brooks Co. Georgia/his great-niece & the G-dau of his sister, Ollie., daughter of HOBSON GOLDMAN and EMMA DAVIS. She was born 03 Nov 1928 in born Thomas County Georgia.

Notes for CAREY FRANKLIN SR. CANNON:
Carey F. Cannon was born July 12, 1894 in either Brooks or Colquitt Co Georgia. He ws the son of George Washington Cannon and MArtha Ann (Susie) Glass Cannon. He is shown in the 1900 Census of the Tallokas District, Brooks Co. Ga. page 2323, as a 5 year old with a birth date of July 1894 and in the 1910 census in militia district # 1445, Autreyville, Colquitt Co. Georgia, page 601, as a 15 year old Farm Hand Living with his parents.

Between the lst marriage and his second marriage; he is known to have had a common law wife with whom he lived 17 years or more. Her name has been reported tohave been Peggy with no last name known. [note by Lavaughn Cannon]

No divorce of the first wife has been found yet but since he remarried in 1946; as shown below and had a common law marriage for more than 17 years; he and his wife were apparently divorced about 1928.

At some point his ex-wife and the children moved to Houston, Texas. After moving to Texas she was known to have had other children and they may have used the name Cannon also even though they were not the children of Carey Cannon. Little else is known of them except that they remained in that area and those surviving along with their descendants were still in that area when last known.

He was a FARMER and in lived in the Brooks Co and Colquitt Co. Georgia area before moving to Houston, Texas. His family lived in Moultrie before moving to Houston, Texas in early 1954 and a few months later this wife left them; and he raised the children alone. They were divorced in January 1961; in Harris County Houston, Texas.

He Retired from Platzer's Shipyard in Houston, Texas. He remained in Houston Texas until October 1963 when he moved to Thomasville, Georgia and remained until his death. He was a Carpenter in his later years.

More About CAREY CANNON and RUTH SIMMONS:
Marriage: 29 Jun 1913, lst wife. Colquitt Co. Georgia

More About CAREY CANNON and WINNIFRED GOLDMAN:
Marriage: 25 Jan 1946, Brooks Co. Georgia/his great-niece & the G-dau of his sister, Ollie.

Children of CAREY CANNON and RUTH SIMMONS are:
    i.   WILLIAM GEORGE[10] CANNON, b. 19 Jul 1915, Moultrie Colquitt Co. Ga.; d. 1984, Houston, Harris Co Tecas/Forest Park Lawndale; m. ? MENN.
    ii.   CHARLES CARMINE CANNON, b. 27 Mar 1919, Thomas, Thomasville, Georgia; d. 29 Jan 1988, Houston Nat'l Cemetery Houston Texas; m. ? ROBERTS.
    iii.   HELEN CANNON.
    iv.   PAULINE "PEGGY" CANNON.
    v.   CAREY FRANKLIN [TWIN] JR CANNON, b. 04 Apr 1927, Georgia; d. 06 Mar 1989, Houston, Harris Co Texas.
    vi.   COREY WILBUR [TWIN] CANNON, b. 04 Apr 1927, Georgia; d. 25 Jul 1984, Houston Harris Texas National Cemetery.

Children of CAREY CANNON and WINNIFRED GOLDMAN are:
73.   vii.   CARRIE LAURETTA[10] CANNON, b. 27 Sep 1946, born Vereen Mem. Hosp., Moultrie Georgia.
    viii.   FRANCES DELORES CANNON, b. 07 Dec 1947.
    ix.   CAREY FRANKLIN JR CANNON, b. 30 Apr 1950.
    x.   RANDY EUGENE CANNON, b. 24 Dec 1952.

57. ELLIS H.[9] CANNON (*REV. GEORGE WASHINGTON*[8], *JOHN CALHOUN*[7], *ARCHIBALD (JR)*[6], *ARCHIBALD "ARCHER" (SR)*[5], *JOHN III*[4], *JOHN*[3], *JOHN*[2], *CANNON FAMILY*[1] *HISTORY*) was born 26 Mar 1902 in Birth date Discrepancy-1900/ Thomasville,Thomas Co. Ga., and died 12 Sep 1973 in Thomas Co., Ga./Sunset Mem. GArdens,Thomasville Ga.. He married LAURA LEE RENTZ 09 Feb 1931 in Thomasville, Thomas Co. Georgia. She was born 02 Aug 1911, and died 10 Mar 1981 in Sunset Mem Gardens/Thomasville, Georgia.

More About ELLIS CANNON and LAURA RENTZ:
Marriage: 09 Feb 1931, Thomasville, Thomas Co. Georgia

Children of ELLIS CANNON and LAURA RENTZ are:
    i.   DOROTHY[10] CANNON.
    ii.   ELLIS LESLEY CANNON.
    iii.   LAVERNE CANNON.
    iv.   CHARLES TRAVIS CANNON.
    v.   GEORGE WESLEY CANNON.

I have much more information on his descendants but I wanted to stop at this generation because it branches out to other surnames: Glass, Croft, Giles, Gray, Bryant, Goldman, and so many more numerous to mention.

My hope is that you will take this information that you now have and add your family lines to it. Keep it growing for many, many generations. God Bless Lanette Hill Brightwell. A descendant of the CANNON family.